S0-DXK-761

THE GREAT TIDING

Interpretation of *Juz' 'Ammā,*
The Last Part of the Qur'ān

Publication of the Islamic Call Society
in Tripoli, Libyan Arab Jamahiriyah
by Mahmoud Ayoub,
Centre for Religious Studies
University of Toronto
1983

© Copyright, 1983
The Islamic Call Society
Tripoli,
The Libyan Arab Jamahiriya

Edited By The Islamic Call Society

LIBRARY OF CONGRESS NUMBER 83-081249

ISBN NUMBER 0-911119-03-5

PRINTED BY: IGRAM PRESS
                 CEDAR RAPIDS, IOWA

PREFACE

The Islamic Call Society in the Libyan Arab Jamahiriyah has produced and distributed translations of Juz' 'Ammā in many languages. The present work was undertaken at the request of the Society to provide the English version of the series. This small volume is presented to the interested reader and the student of Islām in hope that it will be a useful aid for the study of the Qur'ān.

Footnote numbers are made to correspond to the appropriate verse numbers in the hope that this method will provide the reader with a quick and easy reference to the footnotes and the verse or verses to which they relate. A glossary of Arabic terms has been appended to provide the student with an easy reference to the Arabic terms which appear in this volume. I have used the standard American Library of Congress transliteration system with no significant modification. Since this work is meant to be a textbook, every *sūrah* is introduced with a brief discussion of its place in the chronology of the Qur'ān, the occasion of its revelation, and the major themes with which it deals. In order to facilitate reference to the Arabic text which appears side-by side with the English translation, I have strictly followed the verse numbering of the now universally accepted modern Egyptian edition.

Many of the *sūrahs* translated in this volume are commonly used by Muslims in their daily prayers. The actual prayer of Islām, however, is the opening *sūrah (al-Fātiḥah)* of the Qur'ān. I have for this reason decided to close this volume with *Sūrat al-Fātiḥah*.

This work is intended to present *juz' 'ammā* (the thirtieth and last part of the Qur'ān) as directly and straight-forwardly as possible. As will be seen, especially in the general introduction, my purpose is neither to be analytical nor apologetic. I was nevertheless careful to document every major idea or interpretation presented in this work. I alone assume responsibility for the good and the bad in this undertaking, and pray that with all its imperfections, it will be of some use to the students of the Qur'ān, be they Muslim or non-Muslim.

Mahmoud Ayoub

March, 1983

iii

Table of Contents

iv

Introduction

The Qur'ān is for Muslims the word of truth revealed by the Lord of truth to the prophet Muḥammad. It is a book which falsehood does not touch in any way. It was sent down from God to humankind as a remembrance, the preservation of which God has vouchsafed, as He declared in the Qur'ān, "It is We who have sent down the remembrance, and it is We who shall preserve it." (Q. 15:9). It is a book preserved with God, pure and without any blemish, and only those who are truly pure can touch it. Only those who are physically pure may touch it with their hands and tongues, but only those who are pure in heart can truly touch its mysteries and moral and spiritual depths with their minds and inner vision.

The Qur'ān in its essence was from eternity with God: "A glorious Qur'ān in a well-guarded tablet" (Q. 85:22). Yet in its concrete form as a revelation preserved in a book and the hearts of millions of men and women who recite it daily in their prayers and private devotions, the Qur'ān is closely involved in human history. It narrates and analyzes it; it interprets and directs it; and in the end it shall be the basis on which history shall be judged. The Qur'ān is, for Muslims, the foundation of their society and its constitution. It is for this reason that it was sent down in separate portions over a period of twenty or twenty-three years during the prophetic career of Muḥammad, the last messenger of God to humankind. The Qur'ān as a historical document dealt with the real life of a religious community with all its social, economic and political problems. Thus the precepts of the Qur'ān, its moral imperatives and spiritual values which formed the first generation of Muslim society became the norms which nurtured it in its growth into a vibrant world community with a rich and complex religious system and civilization.

The Qur'ān tells us that God "sent it down on the night of determination (*laylat al-qadr*)." It was sent down in its essence as a Divine power to illuminate the dawn of a new era in human history. In its concrete form as a book of guidance to humankind, the Qur'ān was then communicated by God to the Prophet Muḥammad directly through the angel Gabriel. Yet prior to the reception of this awesome message, the rational and spiritual faculties of its recipient had to be prepared for it. Thus before he was called to prophethood, Muḥammad, son of 'Abdallāh son of 'Abd al Muṭṭālib son of Hashim of the tribe of Quraysh was known to his people as al-Amīn, the Trustworthy One. He was a man of mild, quiet nature, of sharp discernment and moral virtue. He never accepted the idol worship of his community, but rather he directed his spiritual and moral energies to the ardent search for the truth. He therefore used to contemplate day and night the signs of God in His creation: the sun, moon, and stars, as well as the life of plants, animals and men. He used, moreover, to spend the month of Ramaḍān of every year in the solitude of a cave on Mount Ḥirā' outside Mecca, the city of his birth. Thus, sharpened by spiritual exercises, Muḥammad's inner vision became attuned to Divine inspiration before he was called to receive and transmit God's messages to His idolatrous people. 'Ā'ishah, the Prophet's wife, related that "the earliest instances of revelation *(waḥī)* to the messenger of God were those of true vision in dreams. He never saw anything in a dream but that it came as clear and true as the break of day". During one of his retreats, when the Prophet was 40 or 43 years of age, the angel Gabriel appeared to him and revealed the first five verses of *Sūrah* 96. This first experience of direct revelation will be recounted at some length in our discussion of that *sūrah*.

After this encounter with the angel Gabriel, there was a brief interruption of revelation which caused the Prophet great sorrow. He was so troubled and filled with uncertainty that he wandered aimlessly in the mountains around Mecca, at times coming close to throwing himself off a high mountain peak. Yet each time the angel would appear to him, saying, "O Muḥammad, you are in truth the messenger of God." This went on for some time until one day, the Prophet is said to have related, "As I was walking, I heard the voice from Heaven. I looked up and saw the angel who came to me in Ḥirā' sitting on a throne between heaven and earth. I was frightened of him; so I ran back to my family saying, 'cover me up! cover me up!' God then sent down, 'O you who are enwrapped! Rise up and warn. Your Lord magnify. Your garments purify and abandon all abomination' (Q. 74: 1-5). After that, revelation began again and continued without interruption".

Whenever the angel of revelation came to the Prophet, he was so affected by it that those around him observed a visible change both in his appearance and actions. The Prophet is himself said to have described his experience as follows: "At times revelation

vii

comes to me like the ringing of a bell. This is the most difficult
[way] for me to endure. When he [the angel] departs from me,
I comprehend what he said. At other times the angel comes to
me in human form and I comprehend what he says". It is further
related on the authority of 'Ā'ishah that, "At times revelation
would come to him, [that is, the Prophet] on a cold winter day,
yet his forehead would be dripping with sweat." It is also related
on the authority of 'Umar b. al-Khaṭṭāb that when revelation
came down to the Prophet, those around him would hear, near
his face, a sound like the buzzing of bees. It is also related that
at the time of revelation the Prophet's face changed and often
he fell into something like a trance and felt as though he was
drawing his last breath. According to some traditions, even his
body became heavy at the moment of revelation so that when
it came to him while on a camel, the beast could hardly support
his weight. ·The Qur'ān is declared to be "weighty speech"
(Q. 73:5). It may be that commentators took this assertion literally or that the change both physical and psychological, in the
Prophet at the time of revelation was so great that it affected
his entire being.

The Prophet began to receive revelation at the age of forty.
After his first encounter with the angel Gabriel who delivered to
him the first five verses of *sūrah* 96, there was an interruption
(*fatrah*) of revelation of two to two-and-a-half years. It is for
this reason that some early authorities asserted that the beginning of revelation was during the Prophet's forty-third year.
After this interruption the Prophet lived in Mecca for ten years,
then migrated to Medina where he also lived for ten years. He
died at the age of sixty-three. Thus the Qur'ān is usually divided
into Meccan and Medinan revelations. This is to say that all the
sūrahs or verses revealed before the migration (*hijrah*) of the
Prophet to Medina are regarded as Meccan even though they
may have been revealed outside the sacred city. Likewise, all the
sūrahs or verses revealed after the *hijrah* are regarded as Medinan
—even those revealed in Mecca itself or any other location during
the travels of the Prophet. It is, however, not possible to determine with certainty what was revealed in Mecca and what in
Medina.

As a general principle, it may be said that all *sūrahs* (except
the second and third) which begin with the unconnected letters
belong to the Meccan period. Those *sūrahs* in which the phrase,

"O you who have faith" occurs are generally considered to be Medinan. In Meccan *sūrahs*, the phrase "O you people (*nās*)" is more commonly used.

The main concern of the Meccan revelations was faith in God and its reward in the hereafter, and rejection of faith (*kufr*) and its dire consequences on the Day of Judgment. In Mecca, the Prophet's role was essentially that of a warner. While the Qur'ān continued in Medina to warn the rejectors of faith of God's punishment and reassure the people of faith of His mercy, still precepts, commands and prohibitions were necessary as the Prophet became the head of a new political entity. Yet the Prophet's political career was not in opposition to his prophetic mission, but complimentary, to and completing it. Another major theme of the Medīnan revelation is human relations in all their aspects: religious, social, political and economic.

Juz' 'ammā (so called because it begins with the words *'ammā* —"about what") consists of a number of short *sūrahs* revealed for the most part in Mecca. We shall indicate the occasion and place of revelation of each *surah* as we study it. This important question has occupied Qur'ān scholars and commentators for centuries.

There is no doubt that the Prophet and his companions used to recite the Qur'ān continuously and study it. We are told in many *hadīth* reports that the angel Gabriel used to review the Qur'ān with the Prophet once a year during the month of Rama-ḍān. It is further related that during the year in which the Prophet died, Gabriel reviewed the Qur'ān with him twice, and this was taken by the Prophet as a sign of his approaching end. The Prophet had a number of scribes known as *katabat al-wahī* (scribes of revelation) who wrote down every verse or *sūrah* as soon as it was delivered by Gabriel to the Prophet. There are many indications that the order of the verses of the Qur'ān, as well as that of some of its *sūrahs*, was set down by the Prophet himself. The final order of the *sūrahs* was set by the committee which was constituted by the third caliph 'Uthmān b. 'Affān to prepare an official recension of the Qur'ān. The Qur'ān is not a book in the sense of a historical or literary document. It is rather a collection of revelations meant to be recited aloud. Even though some of the Prophet's companions, and especially those who served as scribes of revelation, made partial collections which they used in their prayers and private devotions, the art of writing was not so common in Arab society before Islām. Thus the main repository of the Qur'ān was human memory or, to use a well-known expression, "the breasts of men." It was scattered fragments written on stones, palm leaves and parchments made of animal skins that the Qur'ān was finally collected.

Tradition differs as to the time when the first collection of the Qur'ān was made, as well as the person who first suggested such an undertaking. It is not the purpose of this brief introduction to study and analyze the various accounts of this important event in Muslim history. We shall give below the account most-widely accepted, and one which appears to be consciously aimed at harmonizing some of the main views on the subject.

The two years immediately following the death of the Prophet constitute a tumultuous period in the history of the Muslim community. It was a period of internal strife and external danger. The first *khalifāh* (successor) of the Prophet, Abū Bakr, waged a number of wars against those who wished to destroy the community from within by their apostasy from Islām. These wars are known as the wars of *riddah*, that is, wars against apostasy (632-633 A.D.). Abū Bakr had to contend with important external challenges to the new faith by self-proclaimed prophets, most notable among whom was Musaylimah, known in tradition as al-Kadhdhāb (the false prophet). In the war against him (known as the War of Yamāmah) and led by the famous Muslim general Khālid b. al-Walīd, many of the Qur'ān reciters were slain. It was therefore feared that unless the Qur'ān was collected and preserved, it would be lost as death through war and old age claimed its chief bearers.

Tradition tells us that after the War of Yamamah, Abū Bakr and 'Umar called Zāyd b. Thābit, a young man of the Ansār (helpers) of Medina and one of the chief scribes of revelation, and asked him to collect the Qur'an "lest it be lost with the death of its reciters." Zāyd collected the scattered fragments of the Qur'ān from palm leaves, stones, bones and the breasts of men. He then gave the completed text to Ḥafṣah, daughter of 'Umar and wife of the Prophet. This first collection is said to have remained in Ḥafṣah's trust until the death of her father, 'Umar b. al-Khattāb, the second caliph.

We are further told that one of the companions of the Prophet, Hudhayfah b. al-Yamān, came to the third caliph 'Uthmān b. 'Affān, when the latter was occupied with the conquest of Armenia and Adharbayjān and said, "O Commander of the faithful, come to the aid of this community before they differ concerning the Book (that is, the Qur'ān) as did the Jews and Christians differ concerning their books." Hudhayfah based his concern on the past disagreements he observed among the reciters of the Qur'ān in Irāq on what was to be the correct reading of many verses and even long passages of the sacred text. Thus 'Uthmān set up a committee made up of three men of Quraysh and headed by Zāyd b. Thābit to edit and copy the collection of Ḥafṣah. Copies of this official collection, which was henceforth known as the *mushaf* (collection) of 'Uthmān, were then sent to the major centers of the Muslim domain: to Mecca and Yeman in Arabia, Baṣrah and Kūfah in Irāq, and Damascus in Syria, and to Bahrāyn. The Caliph directed that all other copies or fragments of the Qur'ān be destroyed.

According to this account, the Qur'ān was actually collected in the time of Abū Bakr and 'Umar. 'Uthmān only united the community on the use of that early rescension. He did not make a new collection.

Soon, however, the 'Uthmānic recension superseded all others, so that even the collection of Ḥafṣah was burned in order that complete unanimity might be ensured.

The text of the Qur'ān as it was finally fixed in the time of 'Uthmān was still capable of different readings. Such readings *(qirā'āt)* do not, however, appreciably affect the meaning of a verse or phrase. They are mainly concerned with grammatical or dialectical variance. Many readings were current during the early centuries of Islām, but seven have come to be generally accepted and used by Muslims. This may have been in part due to *hadīth* tradition, reported in many versions, which assert that the Qur'ān was sent down according to seven modes, dialects or readings *(ahruf)*.

It is generally held that the order of the verses of the Qur'ān was fixed by the Prophet himself. He often indicated that a certain verse or verses be placed at a specific point in a specific *sūrah*. The companions who were responsible for the task of preparing the official recension of the Qur'ān, perhaps in consultation with others, fixed the order of the *sūrahs*. Generally speaking, this was done according to length of the *sūrahs* rather than chronological order. This is not to say that the time and reason of the revelation of the verses and *sūrahs* of the Qur'ān were of no concern to Muslims. In fact, the occasions *(asbāb)* of the revelation has been the subject of an important branch of Qur'ānic studies.

It has already been observed that Gabriel reviewed the Qur'ān with the Prophet every year in Ramadān. Because of this, it is recommended that people recite the entire Qur'ān during the month of Ramadān. It is also possible that the division of the Qur'ān into thirty equal parts was made in order to facilitate the complete recitation in one month. Completing *(khātm)* of a recitation is in itself considered an act of great merit. Yet the Qur'ān is not intended simply for recitation, however important that may be. Rather, it is a book of guidance to the straight way. It is the only true law and constitution of Muslim society and its sure guide to God and the Good.

The Qur'ān clearly states that God sent the Qur'ān down "in clear Arabic speech" (Q. 26: 195) and that He sent it down "an Arabic Qur'ān" so that men might rationally comprehend its meaning. This means that the Qur'ān can best be studied and understood in its original language. It further means that those who undertake to study and teach the Qur'ān must themselves possess an adequate understanding of the Arabic language: its grammar, philology and usage. Any translation of the Qur'ān can be no more than an approximate interpretation intended only as a tool for the study and understanding of the Arabic text. Recitation of the Qur'ān whether in prayer or general devotions must be in Arabic even if the reciter and his audience have little or no knowledge of the language. Yet because the Qur'ān's teachings are to be understood, pondered and closely adhered to, it is incumbent on every Muslim to learn the language of the Qur'ān. The Qur'ān must speak directly to a Muslim whenever he or she hears its verses. This it can do most effectively in its own language and idiom. It is sincerely hoped that this partial translation will make a small contribution towards a better understanding of the Qur'ān and that it will serve as a stimulus for studying it in its original language.

It has been said that a translation is a betrayal of the original meaning of the text translated. My aim in this work has been to remain as faithful to the original meaning of the text as possible and at the same time to be as clear as possible. If I have succeeded in this task even to a small degree, I thank God for His mercy. If I have failed, I beg His forgiveness for He indeed is All Forgiving, All Merciful.

Sūrah 78
al-Nabā'
(The Awesome Tiding)

This *sūrah* takes its title from the word *al-nabā'* (the awesome tiding) which occurs in the second verse. It consists of forty verses and was revealed late in Mecca. It deals with the following themes:

1. The *sūrah* begins with a statement of the awesome tiding of the Day of Judgment and a warning to humankind of its certainty (verses 1-5).

2. The certainty of the Day of Resurrection is then argued by asserting God's absolute sovereignty over His vast and purposeful creation (verses 6-16).

3. This is followed by a graphic description of the fate of the evil-doers on that day when they shall be made to dwell in the Fire for countless ages (verses 17-30).

4. The fate of these people is then contrasted with the bliss and great pleasures awaiting the righteous people in the Gardens of Paradise (verses 31-36).

5. The *sūrah* ends with yet another assertion of God's sovereignty and absolute dominion over all things and all beings. Before this great majesty the rejectors of faith shall finally discern their insignificance and wish they were dust (verses 37-40).

In the name of God, the All-Merciful, the Compassionate

1. About what do they question one another:

2. about the awesome tiding,

3. concerning which they are in dispute.*

4. No, but they shall indeed know!

5. Again no, indeed they shall soon know!

6. Have we not made the earth a place of repose,

7. and made mountains as pegs [for it]!

8. We created you in pairs.*

9. We made your sleep sound, a time for rest.

10. The night we made as a cloak,*

11. and the day we made a time for livelihood.

12. We erected over you seven strong ones,*

13. and we made a lamp blazing with splendor.*

14. From the rain clouds we send down cascading water,*

15. so that by means of it we bring forth grain and herbs,

16. and gardens dense with foliage.

(v. 1-3) This is a reference to the rejectors of faith of Mecca who denied the resurrection and fell into dispute concerning it among themselves.

(v. 8) That is, males and females.

(v. 10) That is, a cover of darkness for sleep and rest.

(v. 12) That is, the seven heavens or firmaments of the planets.

(v. 13) That is, the sun.

(v. 14) The word *mu'ṣirāt* which we have rendered "rain clouds" had been interpreted by some commentators to mean winds which squeeze out the rain waters from clouds.

(٧٨) سُورَةُ النَّبَإِ مَكِّيَّةٌ وَآيَاتُهَا ٤٠ نَزَلَتْ بَعْدَ الْمَعَارِجِ

بِسْمِ اللهِ الرَّحْمَنِ الرَّحِيمِ

عَمَّ يَتَسَاءَلُونَ ﴿١﴾ عَنِ النَّبَإِ الْعَظِيمِ ﴿٢﴾ الَّذِي هُمْ فِيهِ مُخْتَلِفُونَ ﴿٣﴾ كَلَّا سَيَعْلَمُونَ ﴿٤﴾ ثُمَّ كَلَّا سَيَعْلَمُونَ ﴿٥﴾ أَلَمْ نَجْعَلِ الْأَرْضَ مِهَادًا ﴿٦﴾ وَالْجِبَالَ أَوْتَادًا ﴿٧﴾ وَخَلَقْنَاكُمْ أَزْوَاجًا ﴿٨﴾ وَجَعَلْنَا نَوْمَكُمْ سُبَاتًا ﴿٩﴾ وَجَعَلْنَا اللَّيْلَ لِبَاسًا ﴿١٠﴾ وَجَعَلْنَا النَّهَارَ مَعَاشًا ﴿١١﴾ وَبَنَيْنَا فَوْقَكُمْ سَبْعًا شِدَادًا ﴿١٢﴾ وَجَعَلْنَا سِرَاجًا وَهَّاجًا ﴿١٣﴾ وَأَنْزَلْنَا مِنَ الْمُعْصِرَاتِ مَاءً ثَجَّاجًا ﴿١٤﴾ لِنُخْرِجَ بِهِ حَبًّا وَنَبَاتًا ﴿١٥﴾ وَجَنَّاتٍ أَلْفَافًا ﴿١٦﴾ إِنَّ

17. Surely the day of decision has its appointed time,

18. the day when the trumpets shall sound and you shall all come in droves;*

19. when the heavens shall be opened and become gates,*

20. and the mountains shall be set in motion and become a mirage.

21. Then Hell shall lie in ambush,

22. a place of return for the insolent!

23. In it they shall remain for countless ages.

24. They shall taste therein neither coolness nor any drink,

25. except boiling water and filthy secretions.*

26. A suitable recompense shall it be!

27. This is because they did not expect reckoning;

28. and to our signs, they cried great lies.

29. Yet we accounted everything in a book.

30. Taste, therefore, for we shall not increase you save in torment!

31. As for the God-fearing, they shall have a place of comfort:

32. gardens and vineyards,

33. youthful maidens of like age with firm breasts,

(v. 18) That is, every people, and the messenger who was sent to them. Cf. Q. 17:71.

(v. 19) Through which angels shall descend.

(v. 25) Such as the puss, sweat and tears of the people of Hell.

4

يَوْمَ ٱلْفَصْلِ كَانَ مِيقَٰتًا ۝ يَوْمَ يُنفَخُ فِى ٱلصُّورِ فَتَأْتُونَ

أَفْوَاجًا ۝ وَفُتِحَتِ ٱلسَّمَآءُ فَكَانَتْ أَبْوَٰبًا ۝ وَسُيِّرَتِ

ٱلْجِبَالُ فَكَانَتْ سَرَابًا ۝ إِنَّ جَهَنَّمَ كَانَتْ مِرْصَادًا ۝

لِّلطَّٰغِينَ مَـَٔابًا ۝ لَّٰبِثِينَ فِيهَآ أَحْقَابًا ۝ لَّا يَذُوقُونَ

فِيهَا بَرْدًا وَلَا شَرَابًا ۝ إِلَّا حَمِيمًا وَغَسَّاقًا ۝ جَزَآءً

وِفَاقًا ۝ إِنَّهُمْ كَانُوا۟ لَا يَرْجُونَ حِسَابًا ۝ وَكَذَّبُوا۟

بِـَٔايَٰتِنَا كِذَّابًا ۝ وَكُلَّ شَىْءٍ أَحْصَيْنَٰهُ كِتَٰبًا ۝

فَذُوقُوا۟ فَلَن نَّزِيدَكُمْ إِلَّا عَذَابًا ۝ إِنَّ لِلْمُتَّقِينَ

مَفَازًا ۝ حَدَآئِقَ وَأَعْنَٰبًا ۝ وَكَوَاعِبَ أَتْرَابًا ۝

34. and a cup overflowing;

35. in it, they shall hear neither vain talk nor false-hood.

36. a full recompense from your Lord, a free gift, well-reckoned.*

37. He is the Lord of the heavens and the earth and all that is between them, the All Merciful; with Him they shall have no authority to speak,

38. on a day when angels and the Spirit shall stand in ranks. They shall not speak, except him to whom the All Merciful grants permission and who speaks aright.*

39. That is the day of truth! Let him who will make his final recourse to his Lord.

40. We have surely warned you of a chastisement near at hand. On that day every man shall see what his own hands have sent forth. Then the rejector of faith shall say, "Would that I were dust!"

(v. 36) That is, well-reckoned to satisfy them.

(v. 38) Commentators have differed as to what is meant here by "the Spirit." According to some, it is the spirits of men. Others asserted that they are spirits like those of men but are not human, nor are they angels. Still others interpreted "the Spirit" here to refer to Gabriel. Still another view is that the Spirit here refers to the noblest of the angels and those nearest to God.

وَكَأْسًا دِهَاقًا ﴿٣٤﴾ لَّا يَسْمَعُونَ فِيهَا لَغْوًا وَلَا كِذَّابًا ﴿٣٥﴾

جَزَاءً مِّن رَّبِّكَ عَطَاءً حِسَابًا ﴿٣٦﴾ رَّبِّ السَّمَاوَاتِ

وَالْأَرْضِ وَمَا بَيْنَهُمَا الرَّحْمَـٰنِ لَا يَمْلِكُونَ مِنْهُ خِطَابًا ﴿٣٧﴾

يَوْمَ يَقُومُ الرُّوحُ وَالْمَلَائِكَةُ صَفًّا لَّا يَتَكَلَّمُونَ إِلَّا مَنْ

أَذِنَ لَهُ الرَّحْمَـٰنُ وَقَالَ صَوَابًا ﴿٣٨﴾ ذَٰلِكَ الْيَوْمُ الْحَقُّ

فَمَن شَاءَ اتَّخَذَ إِلَىٰ رَبِّهِ مَآبًا ﴿٣٩﴾ إِنَّا أَنذَرْنَاكُمْ عَذَابًا

قَرِيبًا يَوْمَ يَنظُرُ الْمَرْءُ مَا قَدَّمَتْ يَدَاهُ وَيَقُولُ الْكَافِرُ

يَا لَيْتَنِي كُنتُ تُرَابًا ﴿٤٠﴾

Sūrah 79
al-Nāzi'āt
(Those that Violently Rise or Extract)

This *sūrah* was revealed in Mecca after the previous one and takes its title from the first word, *al-nāzi'āt*. It consists of forty-six verses and may be divided into six sections.

1. The *sūrah* begins (verses 1-5) with a series of oaths wherewith God swears by objects of His own creation. According to most commentators, it is proper for God to swear by anything He created, either for the purpose of showing its greatness or in order to express the awesomeness of what is to follow. The two purposes, however, are not exclusive. It is not proper for men to swear by anything but God, because no one or thing is equal to Him. Thus swearing by any of His creation may be considered as an expression of *shirk* (association of other beings or things with God). In short, God, Who is greater than His creation, may swear by anything He wishes of it, while men can only swear by God alone.

2. Verses 6-14 deal with the doubt of the rejectors of faith of the coming resurrection and describe some of its awesome events and characteristics.

3. The *sūrah* continues (verses 15-26) with the example of Pharaoh's arrogance and transgression and his dealings with the prophet Moses. This is given as a reminder to the prophet Muhammad and his community of God's dealing with ancient peoples and their prophets.

4. This is followed by a challenge to the rejectors of faith to consider God's great wisdom in creation and His power over all things (verses 27-33).

5. The *sūrah* returns (verses 34-41) to the description of the fearful events of the Day of Resurrection. It goes on to contrast the lot of the people of faith with that of the rejectors of faith. The first shall inherit the bliss of Paradise and the second the torments of the Fire.

6. The *sūrah* ends (verses 42-46) with the assertion that knowledge of that dreadful hour is with God alone. Muhammad's task is only to warn humankind of its coming. Yet when it comes, it shall be so real that people will think the time between their death and its coming to have been no more than a night and a day.

In the name of God, the All Merciful, the Compassionate

1. By the extractors vehemently extracting;

2. and those who draw out, violently drawing!

3. By the swimmers incessantly swimming!

4. By the outstrippers, powerfully outstripping;

5. and by those that direct affairs!*

(v. 1-5) Commentators have widely differed regarding the meaning of these five verses. According to classical tradition, *al-nāzi'āt* literally means "extractors" (the angels when they violently extract the souls of men from their bodies). Likewise, *al-nāshitāt* (literally "strong, active or drawing out") are the angels as they draw out the souls, gently causing the dead person to swell with energy or strength *(nashāt)*. Qatādah and Ḥasan al-Basrī, (two important commentators,) interpreted both *al-nāzi'āt* and *al-nāshitāt* to refer to the stars. This interpretation will be discussed more fully below. According to still others, these terms refer to horses in battle. Commentators generally prefer the first view, namely that these are angels of death extracting or drawing out the souls of human beings at the time of death.

As for the swimmers, some said that they are, again, angels swimming, as it were, in the heavens. Others said that they are the stars swimming in their orbits (cf. Q. 36: 40). Still others, taking the words literally, said that the swimmers are the ships swimming in the sea. The outstrippers are, according to some commentators, the angels; according to others, the souls at death. According to still other commentators they are horses in battle. Again, Qatādah asserted that they are the stars outstripping other stars in their orbital motion. Finally, *al-mudabbirāt* (those that direct) are the angels who direct the affairs of the earth in accordance with the command of God and His will. This is the view of most classical commentators.

Some modern comentators interpret all five verses to refer to the stars. *Al-nāzi'āt* are the stars which follow a specific course, such as the sun and moon. *Al-nāshitāt* means the stars moving from one station [*burj*] to another. The swimmers are the stars which move in their spheres serenely as though swimming quietly in water. The outstrippers are those who speedily traverse their course, thus outstripping other stars, such as the moon completing its rotation in one lunar month and the earth in one solar year, and so on. *Al-mudabbirāt* [the directors or managers of the affairs] are the stars which direct the affairs of our earthly world through their influences. Thus the outstripping of the moon teaches us the reckoning of lunar months. In addition, the moon has an important effect on clouds and rainfall as well as the tide. Similarly the outstripping of the sun in its stations teaches us the reckoning of the months. Its movement in completing its annual rotation teaches us

(٧٩) سُورَةُ النَّازِعَاتِ مَكِّيَّة
وَآيَاتُهَا ٤٦ نَزَلَتْ بَعْدَ النَّبَإِ

بِسْمِ اللهِ الرَّحْمَنِ الرَّحِيمِ

وَالنَّازِعَاتِ غَرْقًا ﴿١﴾ وَالنَّاشِطَاتِ نَشْطًا ﴿٢﴾
وَالسَّابِحَاتِ سَبْحًا ﴿٣﴾ فَالسَّابِقَاتِ سَبْقًا ﴿٤﴾ فَالْمُدَبِّرَاتِ

6. On the day when the first convulsion shall convulse [the world],

7. and a second like it shall follow:*

8. on that day, hearts shall be throbbing,

9. their eyes downcast.

10. They shall say, "Are we then to be restored back to life in the grave,*

11. even though we have become dry and hollow bones?"

12. They say, "Surely that is a return availing nothing!"

13. It shall be but a single cry,*

14. and behold, they shall all be awakened.*

---

the reckoning of the years. Thus management of the affairs of the world is attributed to it because of the great benefits contained in its activity.

It may also be that the purpose of mentioning these things in the Qur'ān is first and foremost to create a feeling appropriate to the awesome description of the Day of Resurrection which is to follow. In this case it is not necessary for us to know specifically what such terms mean so long as we live and feel the atmosphere which the Qur'ānic expression seeks to create in many different ways. Thus 'Umar b. al-Khattāb said, after himself regretting questioning the meaning of a verse of the Qur'ān, "Follow those things in the Book which become clear to you, but what does not become clear, let it be."

(v. 6-7) These are the two blasts of the trumpet preceding the resurrection of the dead. The word al-rājifah (that which quakes or convulses) may refer to the earth. The second which shall follow (rādifah) is the quaking of the heaven.

(v. 10) The speakers here are the people of Qurāysh who denied the resurrection. The word ḥāfirah means the pit or grave. It can also mean former state or life. Thus to include both possibilities, I have rendered ḥāfirah as "life in the grave."

(v. 13) According to many commentators, the single cry is the second blast of the trumpet. After the first blast, all living beings shall die and with the second they shall all rise again.

(v. 14) The word sāhirah (awakening) also means "the flat earth." The sense is that after the second blast, all men shall rise up and stand on the flat earth of the final gathering before God for judgment.

أَمْرًا ۝ يَوْمَ تَرْجُفُ ٱلرَّاجِفَةُ ۝ تَتْبَعُهَا ٱلرَّادِفَةُ ۝

قُلُوبٌ يَوْمَئِذٍ وَاجِفَةٌ ۝ أَبْصَٰرُهَا خَٰشِعَةٌ ۝ يَقُولُونَ

أَءِنَّا لَمَرْدُودُونَ فِى ٱلْحَافِرَةِ ۝ أَءِذَا كُنَّا عِظَٰمًا

نَّخِرَةً ۝ قَالُوا تِلْكَ إِذًا كَرَّةٌ خَاسِرَةٌ ۝ فَإِنَّمَا هِىَ زَجْرَةٌ

وَٰحِدَةٌ ۝ فَإِذَا هُم بِٱلسَّاهِرَةِ ۝ هَلْ أَتَىٰكَ حَدِيثُ

15. Has the account of Moses reached you [Muḥammad]?

16. The time when his Lord called out to him in the hallowed valley Ṭuwa:

17. "Go to Pharaoh, for he has waxed arrogant!

18. Say to him, 'Have you the desire to purify yourself

19. and that I guide you to your Lord and that you shall fear [Him]?''

20. Even though he showed him the great sign,

21. still he gave [it] the lie and rebelled.

22. He [Pharoah] then turned away in haste;

23. and gathering [his people], he cried out

24. and proclaimed, 'I am your Lord most high!''

25. But God seized him with the torment of both the next world and this.

26. In this there is indeed a lesson for him who stands in awe [before God].

27. Are you then a greater creation, or the heaven which He built?

28. He lifted up its vault and made good its form.

29. He made dark its night and brought forth its bright day.

30. The earth, after that, He spread out,

مُوسَىٰ ۝ إِذْ نَادَاهُ رَبُّهُۥ بِٱلْوَادِ ٱلْمُقَدَّسِ طُوًى ۝

ٱذْهَبْ إِلَىٰ فِرْعَوْنَ إِنَّهُۥ طَغَىٰ ۝ فَقُلْ هَل لَّكَ إِلَىٰٓ

أَن تَزَكَّىٰ ۝ وَأَهْدِيَكَ إِلَىٰ رَبِّكَ فَتَخْشَىٰ ۝

فَأَرَاهُ ٱلْآيَةَ ٱلْكُبْرَىٰ ۝ فَكَذَّبَ وَعَصَىٰ ۝ ثُمَّ

أَدْبَرَ يَسْعَىٰ ۝ فَحَشَرَ فَنَادَىٰ ۝ فَقَالَ أَنَا۠ رَبُّكُمُ

ٱلْأَعْلَىٰ ۝ فَأَخَذَهُ ٱللَّهُ نَكَالَ ٱلْآخِرَةِ وَٱلْأُولَىٰٓ ۝

إِنَّ فِى ذَٰلِكَ لَعِبْرَةً لِّمَن يَخْشَىٰٓ ۝ ءَأَنتُمْ أَشَدُّ خَلْقًا أَمِ

ٱلسَّمَآءُ بَنَاهَا ۝ رَفَعَ سَمْكَهَا فَسَوَّاهَا ۝ وَأَغْطَشَ

لَيْلَهَا وَأَخْرَجَ ضُحَاهَا ۝ وَٱلْأَرْضَ بَعْدَ ذَٰلِكَ دَحَاهَآ ۝

31. and brought forth from it its waters and pastures.

32. Then the mountains He set firm:

33. [all this] as an enjoyment for you and your flocks.

34. Yet when the great and overwhelming event shall come,

35. on the day when man shall remember what he has striven for,

36. and Hell be displayed for all to see:

37. then he who had acted insolently

38. and preferred the life of this world —

39. Hell shall be [his] dwelling place.

40. But as for him who dreaded the presence of his Lord and forbade the soul its caprice,

41. Paradise shall be his dwelling place.

42. They ask you [Muḥammad] concerning the hour: "When will it come?"

43. Far are you indeed from any knowledge of it!

44. For with your Lord is its determination.

45. You are but a warner to those who stand in awe of it.

46. It shall be, on the day when they see it, as though they had remained [in the grave] only for an evening or [that evening and] the forenoon of the following day.

أَخْرَجَ مِنْهَا مَآءَهَا وَمَرْعَىٰهَا ۝ وَٱلْجِبَالَ أَرْسَىٰهَا ۝

مَتَٰعًا لَّكُمْ وَلِأَنْعَٰمِكُمْ ۝ فَإِذَا جَآءَتِ ٱلطَّآمَّةُ

ٱلْكُبْرَىٰ ۝ يَوْمَ يَتَذَكَّرُ ٱلْإِنسَٰنُ مَا سَعَىٰ ۝

وَبُرِّزَتِ ٱلْجَحِيمُ لِمَن يَرَىٰ ۝ فَأَمَّا مَن طَغَىٰ ۝

وَءَاثَرَ ٱلْحَيَوٰةَ ٱلدُّنْيَا ۝ فَإِنَّ ٱلْجَحِيمَ هِىَ ٱلْمَأْوَىٰ ۝

وَأَمَّا مَنْ خَافَ مَقَامَ رَبِّهِۦ وَنَهَى ٱلنَّفْسَ عَنِ ٱلْهَوَىٰ ۝

فَإِنَّ ٱلْجَنَّةَ هِىَ ٱلْمَأْوَىٰ ۝ يَسْـَٔلُونَكَ عَنِ ٱلسَّاعَةِ أَيَّانَ

مُرْسَىٰهَا ۝ فِيمَ أَنتَ مِن ذِكْرَىٰهَآ ۝ إِلَىٰ رَبِّكَ

مُنتَهَىٰهَآ ۝ إِنَّمَآ أَنتَ مُنذِرُ مَن يَخْشَىٰهَا ۝ كَأَنَّهُمْ

يَوْمَ يَرَوْنَهَا لَمْ يَلْبَثُوٓا۟ إِلَّا عَشِيَّةً أَوْ ضُحَىٰهَا ۝

17

Surah 80
'Abasa
(He Frowned)

This *sūrah* was revealed in Mecca early in the Prophet's mission. It consists of forty-two verses and takes its title from the word, *'abasa* (he frowned), with which the *sūrah* begins. It may be divided into four sections:

1. The first verses (that is, verses 1-10) were revealed concerning a blind man called 'Abdallāh b. Umm Maktūm. Tradition tells us that as the Prophet was one day talking to some of the notables of Quraysh, Ibn Umm Maktūm came to him with some questions, thus interrupting the Prophet's attempt to win the men for the new faith. The Prophet frowned and turned away from the blind man in his anxiety to convince the rich and powerful men. The theme of these verses is, therefore, sincere faith, which must be the criterion of human worth, and not wealth and worldly status.

2. This section (verses 11-16) emphasizes that the foregoing is the basic message of the Qur'ān. It is a reminder to those who truly wish to be admonished. The truth and gravity of this reminder are argued for on the basis of the purity of the Qur'ān itself and the nobility of the angels who are in charge of it.

3. The *sūrah* continues (verses 17-32) with a Divine reproach to man for his arrogant rejection of faith in spite of his insignificant origins and God's bounty towards him.

4. The final section of the *sūrah* (verses 33-42) repeats the familiar warning of the Day of Resurrection with its cataclysmic events. The *sūrah* ends by contrasting the happy state of those who lived righteously with that of the evildoers.

In the name of God, the All Merciful, the Compassionate

1. He frowned and turned away

2. when the blind man approached him.

3. Yet how do you [Muḥammad] know — perhaps
   he would be purified

4. or be reminded, and the remembrance would
   benefit him.

5. But as for him who feels self-sufficient,

6. to him you eagerly attend,

7. though it is not your concern if he does not
   purify himself.

8. But he who eagerly hastens to you,

9. and is in awe [of God],

10. to him you give no heed.

11. No, but it [the Qur'ān] is surely a reminder!

12. Let him therefore who will, remember it.

13. It is contained in high-honored scrolls,

14. lofty and purified,

15. [borne] by the hands of emissaries [angels],

16. noble and righteous.

17. Perish man! How ungrateful he is!

18. Of what did He [God] create him?

19. Out of a drop of sperm He created and deter-
    mined him;

20. then made the way easy for him.

21. He then caused him to die and to be buried.

(٨٠) سُورَةِ عَبَسَ مَكِّيَّةٌ
وَآيَاتُهَا ٤٢ نَزَلَتْ بَعْدَ النَّجْمِ

بِسْمِ اللَّهِ الرَّحْمَنِ الرَّحِيمِ

عَبَسَ وَتَوَلَّى ﴿١﴾ أَن جَاءَهُ الْأَعْمَى ﴿٢﴾ وَمَا يُدْرِيكَ لَعَلَّهُ يَزَّكَّى ﴿٣﴾ أَوْ يَذَّكَّرُ فَتَنفَعَهُ الذِّكْرَى ﴿٤﴾ أَمَّا مَنِ اسْتَغْنَى ﴿٥﴾ فَأَنتَ لَهُ تَصَدَّى ﴿٦﴾ وَمَا عَلَيْكَ أَلَّا يَزَّكَّى ﴿٧﴾ وَأَمَّا مَن جَاءَكَ يَسْعَى ﴿٨﴾ وَهُوَ يَخْشَى ﴿٩﴾ فَأَنتَ عَنْهُ تَلَهَّى ﴿١٠﴾ كَلَّا إِنَّهَا تَذْكِرَةٌ ﴿١١﴾ فَمَن شَاءَ ذَكَرَهُ ﴿١٢﴾ فِي صُحُفٍ مُّكَرَّمَةٍ ﴿١٣﴾ مَّرْفُوعَةٍ مُّطَهَّرَةٍ ﴿١٤﴾ بِأَيْدِي سَفَرَةٍ ﴿١٥﴾ كِرَامٍ بَرَرَةٍ ﴿١٦﴾ قُتِلَ الْإِنسَانُ مَا أَكْفَرَهُ ﴿١٧﴾ مِنْ أَيِّ شَيْءٍ خَلَقَهُ ﴿١٨﴾ مِن نُّطْفَةٍ خَلَقَهُ فَقَدَّرَهُ ﴿١٩﴾ ثُمَّ السَّبِيلَ يَسَّرَهُ ﴿٢٠﴾ ثُمَّ أَمَاتَهُ

21

22. Then when He wills, He raises him.

23. No, indeed, man has not accomplished what He [God] commanded him!*

24. Let man consider his food:

25. We sent down water in pouring rain,

26. then we split the earth into deep furrows.

27. On it we caused grain to grow,

28. grape vines and fresh herbage,

29. olive and palm trees;

30. gardens with trees thick and tall,

31. and fruits and pasture,

32. and enjoyment for you and your flocks.

33. But when the blast shall sound,

34. on the day when a man shall flee from his brother,

35. his mother and his father,

36. his spouse and his children —

37. for every one of them on that day shall have work sufficing him —

38. on that day, there shall be faces radiant,

39. smiling and rejoicing.

40. Other faces on that day shall be covered with dust,

41. overcast with gloom:

42. these are the rejectors of faith, the wicked ones.

(v. 23) Another reading of this verse is, "No, indeed, He[God] has not yet accomplished what He had decreed.

فَأَقْبَرَهُ ﴿٢١﴾ ثُمَّ إِذَا شَاءَ أَنشَرَهُ ﴿٢٢﴾ كَلَّا لَمَّا يَقْضِ

مَا أَمَرَهُ ﴿٢٣﴾ فَلْيَنظُرِ ٱلْإِنسَـٰنُ إِلَىٰ طَعَامِهِ ﴿٢٤﴾ أَنَّا

صَبَبْنَا ٱلْمَاءَ صَبًّا ﴿٢٥﴾ ثُمَّ شَقَقْنَا ٱلْأَرْضَ شَقًّا ﴿٢٦﴾

فَأَنبَتْنَا فِيهَا حَبًّا ﴿٢٧﴾ وَعِنَبًا وَقَضْبًا ﴿٢٨﴾ وَزَيْتُونًا

وَنَخْلًا ﴿٢٩﴾ وَحَدَائِقَ غُلْبًا ﴿٣٠﴾ وَفَٰكِهَةً وَأَبًّا ﴿٣١﴾

مَّتَٰعًا لَّكُمْ وَلِأَنْعَٰمِكُمْ ﴿٣٢﴾ فَإِذَا جَاءَتِ ٱلصَّاخَّةُ ﴿٣٣﴾ يَوْمَ

يَفِرُّ ٱلْمَرْءُ مِنْ أَخِيهِ ﴿٣٤﴾ وَأُمِّهِ وَأَبِيهِ ﴿٣٥﴾ وَصَٰحِبَتِهِ

وَبَنِيهِ ﴿٣٦﴾ لِكُلِّ ٱمْرِئٍ مِّنْهُمْ يَوْمَئِذٍ شَأْنٌ يُغْنِيهِ ﴿٣٧﴾

وُجُوهٌ يَوْمَئِذٍ مُّسْفِرَةٌ ﴿٣٨﴾ ضَاحِكَةٌ مُّسْتَبْشِرَةٌ ﴿٣٩﴾

وَوُجُوهٌ يَوْمَئِذٍ عَلَيْهَا غَبَرَةٌ ﴿٤٠﴾ تَرْهَقُهَا قَتَرَةٌ ﴿٤١﴾

أُوْلَـٰئِكَ هُمُ ٱلْكَفَرَةُ ٱلْفَجَرَةُ ﴿٤٢﴾

23

Sūrah 81
al-Takwīr
(The Folding Up)

This *sūrah* was revealed very early in Mecca after *sūrah* 111, *al-Lahab*, which condemns Abū Lahab, the uncle of the Prophet. It takes its title from the assertion in the first verse that the sun shall be folded up *(kuwwirat)*, the word *takwīr* being the verbal noun. It is related that the Prophet said, "Whoever wishes to look at the Day of Resurrection as if with his own eyes, let him read 'when the sun shall be folded up', 'when the heavens shall be rent' (s. 82), and 'when the heavens shall be split' (s. 84)."

The *sūrah* consists of twenty-nine verses and may be divided into three parts dealing with the following themes:

1. This section (verses 1-14) is a graphic description of the disintegration of nature on the last day, and the appearance of both Hell and Paradise when each shall receive its people. At that time, every soul shall reap the fruits of its actions which it committed here on earth.

2. The second section (verses 15-18) is an oath by the stars, the gathering night and the bursting forth of the morning.

3. This is followed (verses 19-29) with the assertion that the Qur'ān was revealed by God through Gabriel to Muḥammad, who was not a possessed man. The *sūrah* concludes with the familiar warning of the dreadful punishment in the hereafter to those who deny the truths of the resurrection, the Divine source of the Qur'ān and the apostleship of Muḥammad.

In the name of God, the All Merciful, the Compassionate

1. When the sun shall be folded up!*

2. When the stars shall be darkened!

3. When the mountains shall be set in motion!

4. When the ten-month pregnant camels shall be neglected!

5. When the wild beasts shall be brought together!*

6. When the seas shall be set boiling!*

7. When souls shall be coupled!*

8. When the female infant buried alive shall be asked

9. for what sin she was killed.*

10. When the scrolls shall be spread out!

11. When the heavens shall be stripped off!

12. When the Fire shall be set blazing

13. and when Paradise shall be brought near!

14. Then shall every soul know what it has stored up.

15. No, but I swear by the setting stars,

(v. 1) or darkened.

(v. 5) or caused to die.

(v. 6) or intermingle, becoming one vast ocean.

(v. 7) That is, the good with the good and the evil with the evil, or the souls coupled with their bodies.

(v. 9) This verse refers to the pre-Islāmic Arab custom of burying daughters alive so that they would not be captured as concubines and bring dishonor to their family and tribe. Islām absolutely prohibited this custom and, according to tradition, a special expiatory sacrifice was required of those who practised this custom before Islām.

(٨١) سُورَةُ التَّكوِيرِ مَكِّيَّة وَآيَاتُهَا ٢٩ نزلت بَعْدَ المَسَدْ

بِسْمِ اللهِ الرَّحْمَنِ الرَّحِيمِ

إِذَا الشَّمْسُ كُوِّرَتْ ﴿١﴾ وَ إِذَا النُّجُومُ انكَدَرَتْ ﴿٢﴾

وَ إِذَا الْجِبَالُ سُيِّرَتْ ﴿٣﴾ وَ إِذَا الْعِشَارُ عُطِّلَتْ ﴿٤﴾

وَ إِذَا الْوُحُوشُ حُشِرَتْ ﴿٥﴾ وَ إِذَا الْبِحَارُ سُجِّرَتْ ﴿٦﴾

وَ إِذَا النُّفُوسُ زُوِّجَتْ ﴿٧﴾ وَ إِذَا الْمَوْءُودَةُ سُئِلَتْ ﴿٨﴾

بِأَيِّ ذَنبٍ قُتِلَتْ ﴿٩﴾ وَ إِذَا الصُّحُفُ نُشِرَتْ ﴿١٠﴾

وَ إِذَا السَّمَاءُ كُشِطَتْ ﴿١١﴾ وَ إِذَا الْجَحِيمُ سُعِّرَتْ ﴿١٢﴾

وَ إِذَا الْجَنَّةُ أُزْلِفَتْ ﴿١٣﴾ عَلِمَتْ نَفْسٌ مَّا أَحْضَرَتْ ﴿١٤﴾

فَلَا أُقْسِمُ بِالْخُنَّسِ ﴿١٥﴾ الْجَوَارِ الْكُنَّسِ ﴿١٦﴾

27

16. and by those that run [their courses], the rising ones;

17. and by the night when it departs,*

18. and by the morning when it breathes [free from the night]:

19. it is truly the speech of a noble messenger [that is, Gabriel].

20. He is endowed with power, and, with the Lord of the Throne, is of high status.

21. Obeyed is he,* and a faithful trustee.

22. Your companion [Muḥammad] is not possessed

23. for he surely saw him [Gabriel] on the clear horizon!

24. Nor is he [Muḥammad] niggardly with knowledge of that which is concealed.

25. Nor is it [the Qur'ān] the speech of an accursed satan.

26. Where then will you be able to go!

27. It [the Qur'ān] is but a reminder for humankind,

28. for him among you who wills to be guided aright.

29. Yet you shall not will unless God wills, the Lord of all beings.

(v. 17) Or comes on.

(v. 21) That is, in heaven by the angels.

وَٱلَّيْلِ إِذَا عَسْعَسَ ۝ وَٱلصُّبْحِ إِذَا تَنَفَّسَ ۝

إِنَّهُۥ لَقَوْلُ رَسُولٍ كَرِيمٍ ۝ ذِى قُوَّةٍ عِندَ ذِى ٱلْعَرْشِ

مَكِينٍ ۝ مُّطَاعٍ ثَمَّ أَمِينٍ ۝ وَمَا صَاحِبُكُم

بِمَجْنُونٍ ۝ وَلَقَدْ رَءَاهُ بِٱلْأُفُقِ ٱلْمُبِينِ ۝ وَمَا هُوَ عَلَى

ٱلْغَيْبِ بِضَنِينٍ ۝ وَمَا هُوَ بِقَوْلِ شَيْطَانٍ رَّجِيمٍ ۝

فَأَيْنَ تَذْهَبُونَ ۝ إِنْ هُوَ إِلَّا ذِكْرٌ لِّلْعَالَمِينَ ۝ لِمَن

شَاءَ مِنكُمْ أَن يَسْتَقِيمَ ۝ وَمَا تَشَاءُونَ إِلَّا أَن يَشَاءَ

ٱللَّهُ رَبُّ ٱلْعَالَمِينَ ۝

Sūrah 82
al-Infiṭār
(The Rending)

This sūrah was revealed in Mecca after *Surah* 79 *(al-nāzi ʿāt)*. It takes its title from the verb in the first verse *(infaṭarat)*, describing heaven being rent. It consists of nineteen verses and may be divided into four sections.

1. The first section (verses 1-5) is a vivid description of the upheavals in the heavens and in nature accompanying the Day of Resurrection.

2. The second part (verses 6-8) is a Divine reproach to man for his ingratitude and wickedness in the face of God's high favor towards him.

3. The third section (verses 9-12) addresses human beings in general, reproaching them for denying the truth of faith and the rewards and punishments on the Last Day. They are warned that God has set up angels over them to watch and record their deeds.

4. The final section (verses 13-19) contrasts the bliss of the righteous in Paradise with the torments of the wicked in the Fire. The *sūrah* concludes with an affirmation of God's sovereignty on the Day of Judgment.

In the name of God the All Merciful, the Compassionate

1. When the heaven shall be rent!

2. When the stars shall be scattered!

3. When the seas shall burst together!*

4. When the graves shall be overturned:

5. then every soul shall know what it has sent forth and what it has neglected.*

6. O man, what was it that deceived you concerning your magnanimous Lord,

7. who created you, shaped you and formed you in just proportions?

8. In whatever form He wished, He formed you.*

9. No, rather you give the lie to the [Day of] Judgment.

10. Yet over you stand watchers,*

11. noble scribes

12. who know whatever you do.

13. Surely the righteous shall be in bliss,*

14. while the wicked shall be in a blazing Fire.

15. In it they shall burn on the Day of Judgment,

16. nor will they ever be absent from it.

(v. 3) i.e., the sweet with the salty water.

(v. 5) i.e., sent forth good deeds and neglected to do so by not being diligent in this world in doing good.

(v.8) The words "In whatever form He wished" may mean that God was able to create man in a most marvellous form (p. 65).

(v. 10) i.e., angels.

(v. 13) i.e., in Paradise.

(٨٢) سُورَةُ الأنفِطَارِ مَكِّيَّة
وَآياتُها ١٩ نَزَلَتْ بَعْدَ النَّازِعَاتِ

بِسْمِ اللهِ الرَّحْمَنِ الرَّحِيمِ

إِذَا السَّمَاءُ انفَطَرَتْ ۝ وَإِذَا الكَوَاكِبُ انتَثَرَتْ ۝ وَإِذَا البِحَارُ فُجِّرَتْ ۝ وَإِذَا القُبُورُ بُعْثِرَتْ ۝ عَلِمَتْ نَفْسٌ مَّا قَدَّمَتْ وَأَخَّرَتْ ۝ يَا أَيُّهَا الإِنسَانُ مَا غَرَّكَ بِرَبِّكَ الكَرِيمِ ۝ الَّذِي خَلَقَكَ فَسَوَّاكَ فَعَدَلَكَ ۝ فِي أَيِّ صُورَةٍ مَّا شَاءَ رَكَّبَكَ ۝ كَلَّا بَلْ تُكَذِّبُونَ بِالدِّينِ ۝ وَإِنَّ عَلَيْكُمْ لَحَافِظِينَ ۝ كِرَامًا كَاتِبِينَ ۝ يَعْلَمُونَ مَا تَفْعَلُونَ ۝ إِنَّ الأَبْرَارَ لَفِي نَعِيمٍ ۝ وَإِنَّ الفُجَّارَ لَفِي جَحِيمٍ ۝ يَصْلَوْنَهَا يَوْمَ الدِّينِ ۝ وَمَا هُمْ عَنْهَا بِغَائِبِينَ ۝

33

17. Would that you knew what the Day of Judgment is!

18. Again would that you knew what the Day of Judgment is!

19. A day when no soul shall possess anything with which to benefit another soul, for on that day the matter shall belong entirely to God.*

(v. 19) i.e., sovereignty on that day shall belong only to God.

وَمَآ أَدۡرَىٰكَ مَا يَوۡمُ ٱلدِّينِ ﴿١٧﴾ ثُمَّ مَآ أَدۡرَىٰكَ مَا يَوۡمُ ٱلدِّينِ ﴿١٨﴾ يَوۡمَ لَا تَمۡلِكُ نَفۡسٌ لِّنَفۡسٍ شَيۡـًٔا ۖ وَٱلۡأَمۡرُ يَوۡمَئِذٍ لِّلَّهِ ﴿١٩﴾

Sūrah 83
al-Muṭaffifīn
(Those Who Give Short Measure)

This *sūrah* was the last to be revealed in Mecca save for perhaps the first four verses, which may have been revealed shortly after the Prophet's arrival in Medina. The *sūrah* consists of thirty-six verses and takes its title from the word *mutaffifīn* (those who give short measure) mentioned in the first verse.

The present *sūrah* may be divided into four parts and deals with the following themes:

1. It opens with a threat and a reminder to those who deceive others in their commercial dealings by giving short measure. They do so, yet they insist on exact measures for themselves (verses 1-6).

2. The second part (verses 7-17) declares that the book of the deeds of the wicked is in the lowest station. This is to say that their deeds shall inevitably lead them to the lowest place, which is Hell. This shall be their punishment for denying the truth of the Qur'ān, which they consider to be simply ancient legends.

3. The third section (verses 18-28) declares, in contrast, that the book of the deeds of the righteous is in exalted stations. Their great bliss is likewise contrasted with the torment of the wicked on the Day of Judgment.

4. The *sūrah* goes on (verses 29-36) to give a more general picture of the sinners here on earth who mocked and despised the people of faith, and of how they in turn shall be mocked by the same people. The former will endure great torment and mental anguish, while the righteous will enjoy great bliss and peace.

In the name of God, the All-Merciful, the Compassionate

1. Woe to those who give short measure,

2. those who when measuring for themselves against other people take their full due.

3. But when they measure or weigh things for others, they give short measure.

4. Do these people not think that they shall be raised from the dead

5. for an awesome day,

6. a day when all men shall stand before the Lord of all beings?

7. No, indeed, the book of the wicked shall be in *sijjīn.**

8. Would that you knew what *sijjīn* is!

9. It is a book inscribed.*

10. Woe on that day to those who cry lies,

11. those who cry lies concerning the Day of Judgment.

12. Yet no one cries lies concerning it except he who is a transgressor, a sinner.

13. When our revelations are recited to him, he says, "These are merely tales of the ancients."

(v. 7) The word *sijjīn* is an intensive form of the word *sajana,* meaning "to imprison." The sense is, therefore, that the record of the deeds of the wicked shall lead them to the lowest place, a place from which there is no escape.

(v. 9) This verse is not an answer to the previous one. Rather, it continues the idea in verse 7 and describes the book of the wicked, not *sijjīn.*

(٨٣) سُورَةُ المُطَفِّفِينَ مَكِّيَّةٌ
وَآيَاتُهَا ٣٦ نَزَلَتْ بَعْدَ العَنْكَبُوت
وَهِيَ آخِرُ سُورَةٍ نَزَلَتْ بِمَكَّة

بِسْمِ اللَّهِ الرَّحْمَٰنِ الرَّحِيمِ

وَيْلٌ لِّلْمُطَفِّفِينَ ﴿١﴾ الَّذِينَ إِذَا اكْتَالُوا عَلَى النَّاسِ يَسْتَوْفُونَ ﴿٢﴾ وَإِذَا كَالُوهُمْ أَو وَّزَنُوهُمْ يُخْسِرُونَ ﴿٣﴾ أَلَا يَظُنُّ أُولَٰئِكَ أَنَّهُم مَّبْعُوثُونَ ﴿٤﴾ لِيَوْمٍ عَظِيمٍ ﴿٥﴾ يَوْمَ يَقُومُ النَّاسُ لِرَبِّ الْعَالَمِينَ ﴿٦﴾ كَلَّا إِنَّ كِتَابَ الْفُجَّارِ لَفِي سِجِّينٍ ﴿٧﴾ وَمَا أَدْرَاكَ مَا سِجِّينٌ ﴿٨﴾ كِتَابٌ مَّرْقُومٌ ﴿٩﴾ وَيْلٌ يَوْمَئِذٍ لِّلْمُكَذِّبِينَ ﴿١٠﴾ الَّذِينَ يُكَذِّبُونَ بِيَوْمِ الدِّينِ ﴿١١﴾ وَمَا يُكَذِّبُ بِهِ إِلَّا كُلُّ مُعْتَدٍ أَثِيمٍ ﴿١٢﴾ إِذَا تُتْلَىٰ عَلَيْهِ آيَاتُنَا قَالَ أَسَاطِيرُ الْأَوَّلِينَ ﴿١٣﴾

14. No, indeed, that which they have earned has as rust covered their hearts.

15. No, indeed on that day they shall be veiled from their Lord;

16. then they shall burn in a blazing Fire.

17. Then it shall be said to them, "This is that to which you cried lies!"

18. No, indeed, the book of the righteous shall be in *'illiyīn*.*

19. Would that you knew what *'illiyīn is!*

20. A book inscribed,*

21. witnessed by those brought near [to God].

22. Surely the righteous shall be in bliss,

23. upon couches, gazing.*

24. In their faces you recognize the radiance of bliss.

25. They shall be given a sealed wine to drink;

26. its seal shall be of musk. Then after this let the strivers strive.

27. Its blend shall be of Tasnīm,*

(v. 18) The word *'illiyīn* is an intensive form of the root *'alā* meaning "to rise up high." It is a plural of the word *'illi*, meaning "highest." Thus it is the opposite of *sijjīn*. According to classical tradition, *sijjīn* is beneath the seventh earth, while *'illiyīn* is in the seventh heaven.

(v. 20) See note to v. 9, above.

(v. 23) The righteous in Paradise shall gaze upon their Lord as the wicked will be veiled from Him. It has also been said that "gazing" here means gazing on their own vast domains in Paradise. The first view, however, is more widely accepted as it is more in harmony with the context of the entire passage.

(v. 27) Tasnīm is a spring of the water of Paradise running down from a high place. It is the noblest drink of Paradise.

كَلَّا بَلْ رَانَ عَلَى قُلُوبِهِم مَّا كَانُوا يَكْسِبُونَ ﴿١٤﴾ كَلَّا إِنَّهُمْ عَن رَّبِّهِمْ يَوْمَئِذٍ لَّمَحْجُوبُونَ ﴿١٥﴾ ثُمَّ إِنَّهُمْ لَصَالُوا الْجَحِيمِ ﴿١٦﴾ ثُمَّ يُقَالُ هَٰذَا الَّذِي كُنتُم بِهِ تُكَذِّبُونَ ﴿١٧﴾ كَلَّا إِنَّ كِتَابَ الْأَبْرَارِ لَفِي عِلِّيِّينَ ﴿١٨﴾ وَمَا أَدْرَاكَ مَا عِلِّيُّونَ ﴿١٩﴾ كِتَابٌ مَّرْقُومٌ ﴿٢٠﴾ يَشْهَدُهُ الْمُقَرَّبُونَ ﴿٢١﴾ إِنَّ الْأَبْرَارَ لَفِي نَعِيمٍ ﴿٢٢﴾ عَلَى الْأَرَائِكِ يَنظُرُونَ ﴿٢٣﴾ تَعْرِفُ فِي وُجُوهِهِمْ نَضْرَةَ النَّعِيمِ ﴿٢٤﴾ يُسْقَوْنَ مِن رَّحِيقٍ مَّخْتُومٍ ﴿٢٥﴾ خِتَامُهُ مِسْكٌ وَفِي ذَٰلِكَ فَلْيَتَنَافَسِ الْمُتَنَافِسُونَ ﴿٢٦﴾ وَمِزَاجُهُ مِن تَسْنِيمٍ ﴿٢٧﴾ عَيْنًا يَشْرَبُ بِهَا الْمُقَرَّبُونَ ﴿٢٨﴾ إِنَّ الَّذِينَ

28. a spring from which those who are brought near shall drink.

29. The sinners did laugh at the people of faith,

30. and when they passed by them, they winked at one another;

31. when they returned to their people, they were full of merriment.

32. When they saw them they said, "These people have indeed gone astray!"

33. Yet they were not sent as watchers over them.

34. And this day, those who have faith are laughing at the rejectors of faith.

35. They are upon couches, gazing.*

36. Have then the rejectors of faith been rewarded for what they have done?

(v. 35) This is an answer to the claim of the sinners that the people of faith were in error. Rather they shall be brought near to God on the day of resurrection and will gaze upon Him.

أَجْرَمُواْ كَانُواْ مِنَ ٱلَّذِينَ ءَامَنُواْ يَضْحَكُونَ ۩ وَإِذَا

مَرُّواْ بِهِمْ يَتَغَامَزُونَ ۩ وَإِذَا ٱنقَلَبُوٓاْ إِلَىٰٓ أَهْلِهِمُ

ٱنقَلَبُواْ فَكِهِينَ ۩ وَإِذَا رَأَوْهُمْ قَالُوٓاْ إِنَّ هَٰٓؤُلَآءِ

لَضَآلُّونَ ۩ وَمَآ أُرْسِلُواْ عَلَيْهِمْ حَٰفِظِينَ ۩

فَٱلْيَوْمَ ٱلَّذِينَ ءَامَنُواْ مِنَ ٱلْكُفَّارِ يَضْحَكُونَ ۩ عَلَى

ٱلْأَرَآئِكِ يَنظُرُونَ ۩ هَلْ ثُوِّبَ ٱلْكُفَّارُ مَا كَانُواْ

يَفْعَلُونَ ۩

Sūrah 84
al-Inshiqāq
(The Splitting)

This *sūrah* was revealed in Mecca after *sūrah* 82, *al-Infiṭār*. It consists of twenty-five verses. It is related that Abu Hurayrah (a well-known Companion and *ḥadīth* transmitter) used to prostrate himself at the conclusion of the recitation of this *sūrah*. When asked concerning this, he replied, "I prostrated myself behind Abū al-Qāsim [i.e., the Prophet] and I shall continue to prostrate myself after reciting it until I meet him".

The *sūrah* may be divided into four parts and deals with the following themes:

1. It begins with a dramatic depiction of the events of the Day of Resurrection (verses 1-5).

2. Man is reminded of his own condition on that day when he shall either be given the book of his deeds in his right hand and be happy, or in his left hand (behind his back) and be condemned (verses 6-15).

3. An oath by the twilight, the night and moon is followed by the assertion that human beings endure different conditions in this life and after death (verses 16-19).

4. The *sūrah* ends with a warning of punishment to the rejectors of faith for not heeding the Qur'ān, and glad tidings for the people of faith of an unending reward (verses 20-25).

In the name of God the All Merciful, the Compassionate

1. When the heaven shall be split,

2. and give ear to its Lord, as in truth it must!

3. When the earth shall be spread out,

4. and cast out what is in it and void itself,

5. and give ear to its Lord, as indeed it must!

6. O Man, you are indeed toiling towards your Lord laboriously, and you shall meet Him.

7. As for him who shall be given his book in his right hand,

8. he shall be brought to answer, but with an easy reckoning.

9. He shall return to his kinsfolk, rejoicing.*

10. But as for him who shall be given his book behind his back,*

11. he shall cry out perdition (upon himself),

12. and shall burn in a blazing Fire.

13. He was, before, happy among his people;

14. he surely thought he would never return [to God].

15. Yet his Lord has indeed seen him.

16. No, but I swear by the twilight!

17. By the night when it envelopes [all things in darkness]

(v. 9) According to early commentators, he shall return to his kinsfolk in Paradise.

(v. 10) i.e., in his left hand.

(٨٤) سُورَةُ الأَنْشِقَاقِ مَكِّيَّة
وَآيَاتُهَا ٢٥ نَزَلَتْ بَعْدَ الأَنْفِطَارِ

بِسْمِ اللهِ الرَّحْمٰنِ الرَّحِيمِ

إِذَا السَّمَاءُ انْشَقَّتْ ﴿١﴾ وَأَذِنَتْ لِرَبِّهَا وَحُقَّتْ ﴿٢﴾

وَإِذَا الأَرْضُ مُدَّتْ ﴿٣﴾ وَأَلْقَتْ مَا فِيهَا وَتَخَلَّتْ ﴿٤﴾

وَأَذِنَتْ لِرَبِّهَا وَحُقَّتْ ﴿٥﴾ يَا أَيُّهَا الإِنْسَنُ إِنَّكَ كَادِحٌ

إِلَى رَبِّكَ كَدْحًا فَمُلَٰقِيهِ ﴿٦﴾ فَأَمَّا مَنْ أُوتِيَ كِتَٰبَهُ

بِيَمِينِهِ ﴿٧﴾ فَسَوْفَ يُحَاسَبُ حِسَابًا يَسِيرًا ﴿٨﴾

وَيَنقَلِبُ إِلَى أَهْلِهِ مَسْرُورًا ﴿٩﴾ وَأَمَّا مَنْ أُوتِيَ كِتَٰبَهُ

وَرَاءَ ظَهْرِهِ ﴿١٠﴾ فَسَوْفَ يَدْعُواْ ثُبُورًا ﴿١١﴾ وَيَصْلَى

سَعِيرًا ﴿١٢﴾ إِنَّهُ كَانَ فِي أَهْلِهِ مَسْرُورًا ﴿١٣﴾ إِنَّهُ ظَنَّ أَن

لَّن يَحُورَ ﴿١٤﴾ بَلَىٰ إِنَّ رَبَّهُ كَانَ بِهِ بَصِيرًا ﴿١٥﴾ فَلَا أُقْسِمُ

18. and the moon when it is full:

19. surely you shall endure one condition after another.*

20. Why, then, do they not have faith,

21. and when the Qur'ān is recited to them, do they not fall prostrate?

22. Rather those who have rejected faith cry lies,

23. yet God knows well what they conceal.

24. So give them good tidings of a painful torment!*

25. But as for those who have faith and perform good deeds, theirs shall be a reward unending.

(v. 19) According to most commentators this verse is addressed to Muslims who have to endure successive conditions of hardship in this and the next world. The verse has also been read in the singular as addressed to the Prophet Muḥammad: "You shall rise [on the night of the heavenly journey, that is, the *mi'rāj*] from one heaven to another." The first view, however, is the accepted one, as it is based on the more generally accepted reading of the verse.

(v. 24) The word *bashirhum* (give them glad tidings) is here used mockingly.

بِالشَّفَقِ ﴿١٦﴾ وَالَّيْلِ وَمَا وَسَقَ ﴿١٧﴾ وَالْقَمَرِ إِذَا اتَّسَقَ ﴿١٨﴾

لَتَرْكَبُنَّ طَبَقًا عَن طَبَقٍ ﴿١٩﴾ فَمَا لَهُمْ لَا يُؤْمِنُونَ ﴿٢٠﴾

وَإِذَا قُرِئَ عَلَيْهِمُ الْقُرْءَانُ لَا يَسْجُدُونَ ۩ ﴿٢١﴾ بَلِ الَّذِينَ

كَفَرُوا يُكَذِّبُونَ ﴿٢٢﴾ وَاللَّهُ أَعْلَمُ بِمَا يُوعُونَ ﴿٢٣﴾ فَبَشِّرْهُم

بِعَذَابٍ أَلِيمٍ ﴿٢٤﴾ إِلَّا الَّذِينَ ءَامَنُوا وَعَمِلُوا الصَّالِحَاتِ

لَهُمْ أَجْرٌ غَيْرُ مَمْنُونٍ ﴿٢٥﴾

Sūrah 85
al-Burūj
(The Constellations)

This *sūrah* consists of twenty-two verses and was revealed in Mecca after *sūrah* 91, *al-Shams*. The *sūrah* may be divided into six sections.

1. The first section (verses 1-3) is an oath by the constellations or signs of the zodiac, by the Day of Resurrection, and by the creation witnessing it.

2. The second section alludes to the story of the people of the pit, to be discussed below (verses 4-9).

3. A further comment (verses 10-11) on all those who persecute the people of faith and do not subsequently repent, follows.

4. The fourth section (verses 12-16) continues the same theme by stressing God's awesome power against the wicked, and love and mercy towards the righteous.

5. The fifth section (verses 17-20) provides two well-known examples of human folly and arrogance, Pharaoh of Egypt who rejected the prophet Moses, and the ancient Arab tribe of Thamūd who rejected Sālih, God's messenger to them.

6. The *sūrah* ends (verses 21-22) with the assertion that the Qur'ān is a glorious revelation preserved by God in the well-guarded, Tablet.

This and the following *sūrah* are recommended to be recited in the night prayers, following the example of the Prophet as reported by Abū Hurayrah.

In the name of God the All Merciful, the Compassionate

1. By the heaven with its constellations!

2. By the promised day!*

3. By the witness and that which is witnessed!*

4. Cursed are the people of the pit!*

5. It was a fire blazing with fuel,

6. when they sat over it.*

(v. 2) i.e., the Day of Resurrection, according to most commentators.

(v. 3) Commentators have widely differed in their interpretation of this verse. Many views have been offered.

(a) The first view is that the witness is Friday and that the witnessed is the day of ʿArafāh, the last day of the pilgrimmage.

(b) According to some commentators, the witness is the Day of Resurrection which will be witnessed by all creatures.

(c) It was related that Ḥasan, son of ʿAlī, interpreted the witness to mean Muḥammad. In support of this interpretation he quoted the verse, "How would it then be if we were to bring forth (on the Day of Resurrection) a witness from every community and bring you forth as a witness over these people (i.e., the Muslims)" (Q. 4: 41). The witnessed, according to this interpretation, is the Day of Resurrection.

(d) According to Ibn ʿAbbās (the foremost authority on Qurʾānic interpretation) the witness is God and the witnessed is the Day of Resurrection.

Modern commentators took a less complex approach, according to which the witness and the witnessed are all the things God created in this universe. This is because everything he created witnesses to the majesty of His power and great wisdom. It is also witnessed by everyone who has eyes to see.

(v. 4) Commentators have related a number of stories and legends identifying the people of the pit. Some modern commentators do not identify them but take the reference to be to some unknown people. Classical commentators accept the view that the people of the pit are the Yeminite Jewish King Dhu al-Nawwas and his people, who dug pits, filled them with fire, and threw into them the Christian martyrs of Najran (a well known city in ancient Arabia).

(v. 5-6) i.e., the persecutors who sat over the fire witnessing the people of faith being consumed by it.

52

(٨٥) سُورَةُ البُرُوجِ مَكِّيّة وَآياتُها ٢٢ نزلَت بَعدَ الشَّمسِ

بِسْمِ اللهِ الرَّحْمٰنِ الرَّحِيمِ

وَالسَّمَاءِ ذَاتِ الْبُرُوجِ ﴿١﴾ وَالْيَوْمِ الْمَوْعُودِ ﴿٢﴾

وَشَاهِدٍ وَمَشْهُودٍ ﴿٣﴾ قُتِلَ أَصْحَابُ الْأُخْدُودِ ﴿٤﴾

النَّارِ ذَاتِ الْوَقُودِ ﴿٥﴾ إِذْ هُمْ عَلَيْهَا قُعُودٌ ﴿٦﴾ وَهُمْ

عَلَىٰ مَا يَفْعَلُونَ بِالْمُؤْمِنِينَ شُهُودٌ ﴿٧﴾ وَمَا نَقَمُوا مِنْهُمْ

7. They were themselves witnesses of what they did to the people of faith.

8. Yet they found no blame in them except that they had faith in God, the Almighty, the All Praised,

9. to Whom belongs dominion of the heavens and the earth; and God is witness over all things.

10. Surely those who persecuted the men and women of faith and did not repent thereafter: theirs shall be the torment of Hell, and theirs shall be the torment of burning.

11. But as for those who have faith and do good deeds, there await them gardens beneath which rivers flow; this indeed is the great triumph.

12. Terrible indeed is the force of your Lord!

13. He it is who originates and brings back to life.

14. He is the All Forgiving, the All Loving,

15. Lord of the glorious throne,

16. doer of whatever He wills.

17. Has the account of the hosts come to you,

18. Pharaoh and Thamūd?*

19. Rather, those who have rejected faith persist in crying lies.

20. But God is behind them, All Encompassing.

21. This surely is a glorious Qur'ān,

22. preserved in a well-guarded Tablet.

(v. 18) i.e., Pharaoh and his helpers (who are called troops here) and Thamūd, an ancient Arab tribe to whom the prophet Ṣāliḥ was sent; but they rejected his message.

إِلَّا أَن يُؤْمِنُواْ بِٱللهِ ٱلْعَزِيزِ ٱلْحَمِيدِ ﴿٨﴾ ٱلَّذِى لَهُۥ مُلْكُ

ٱلسَّمَٰوَٰتِ وَٱلْأَرْضِ ۚ وَٱللهُ عَلَىٰ كُلِّ شَىْءٍ شَهِيدٌ ﴿٩﴾

إِنَّ ٱلَّذِينَ فَتَنُواْ ٱلْمُؤْمِنِينَ وَٱلْمُؤْمِنَٰتِ ثُمَّ لَمْ يَتُوبُواْ

فَلَهُمْ عَذَابُ جَهَنَّمَ وَلَهُمْ عَذَابُ ٱلْحَرِيقِ ﴿١٠﴾ إِنَّ

ٱلَّذِينَ ءَامَنُواْ وَعَمِلُواْ ٱلصَّٰلِحَٰتِ لَهُمْ جَنَّٰتٌ تَجْرِى مِن

تَحْتِهَا ٱلْأَنْهَٰرُ ۚ ذَٰلِكَ ٱلْفَوْزُ ٱلْكَبِيرُ ﴿١١﴾ إِنَّ بَطْشَ رَبِّكَ

لَشَدِيدٌ ﴿١٢﴾ إِنَّهُۥ هُوَ يُبْدِئُ وَيُعِيدُ ﴿١٣﴾ وَهُوَ ٱلْغَفُورُ

ٱلْوَدُودُ ﴿١٤﴾ ذُو ٱلْعَرْشِ ٱلْمَجِيدُ ﴿١٥﴾ فَعَّالٌ لِّمَا

يُرِيدُ ﴿١٦﴾ هَلْ أَتَىٰكَ حَدِيثُ ٱلْجُنُودِ ﴿١٧﴾ فِرْعَوْنَ

وَثَمُودَ ﴿١٨﴾ بَلِ ٱلَّذِينَ كَفَرُواْ فِى تَكْذِيبٍ ﴿١٩﴾ وَٱللهُ

مِن وَرَآئِهِم مُّحِيطٌ ﴿٢٠﴾ بَلْ هُوَ قُرْءَانٌ مَّجِيدٌ ﴿٢١﴾

فِى لَوْحٍ مَّحْفُوظٍ ﴿٢٢﴾

Sūrah 86
al-Ṭāriq
(The Night Star)

This *sūrah* was revealed early in Mecca after *sūrah* 90, *al-Balad*. It takes its title from the word *al-ṭāriq* (the night star) mentioned in the first verse. It has already been observed that the Prophet recommended that this and the previous *sūrah* be recited in the night prayers. The *sūrah* consists of seventeen verses and may be divided into three parts.

1. The *sūrah* begins (verses 1-4) with an oath by the heaven and its luminaries, followed by the assertion that every soul has a watching angel set over it.

2. The second part (verses 5-10) is a reminder to man of his lowly origins and a warning that on the Day of Resurrection he shall stand before God, having neither strength nor helper.

3. The final section (verses 11-17) begins with an oath by the heaven with its rains, and the earth bursting with life made possible through this rain. This is followed by the assertion that the Qur'ān in general, and the truth expressed in this *sūrah* in particular, is a decisive word, not spoken in jest. The *sūrah* concludes with an assertion of God's absolute knowledge and control over what the rejectors of faith do.

In the name of God the All Merciful, the Compassionate

1. By the heaven and the night star:

2. would that you knew what the night star is —

3. the piercing star.

4. Surely over every soul there is a watcher.

5. Let man then consider of what he was created.

6. He was created of gushing water;*

7. he issues from between the loins and the breast bones.*

8. He [God] is surely able to bring him back [to life],

9. on a day when all innermost thoughts shall be revealed.

10. Then he shall have neither strength nor helper.

11. By the heaven with its returning rains!

12. By the earth splitting [with plants]:

13. it is surely a decisive word;

14. it is not uttered in jest.

15. They are devising great schemes,

16. and I am myself devising great schemes!

17. Then let the rejectors of faith have respite; let them have a brief respite!

(v. 6) i.e., the seminal fluid.
(v. 7) of woman.

(٨٦) سُورَةُ الطّارقِ مكّية
وآياتُها ١٧ نزلت بَعدَ البَلَد

بِسْمِ اللَّهِ الرَّحْمَنِ الرَّحِيمِ

وَالسَّمَاءِ وَالطَّارِقِ ﴿١﴾ وَمَا أَدْرَىٰكَ مَا الطَّارِقُ ﴿٢﴾

النَّجْمُ الثَّاقِبُ ﴿٣﴾ إِن كُلُّ نَفْسٍ لَّمَّا عَلَيْهَا حَافِظٌ ﴿٤﴾

فَلْيَنظُرِ الْإِنسَـٰنُ مِمَّ خُلِقَ ﴿٥﴾ خُلِقَ مِن مَّاءٍ دَافِقٍ ﴿٦﴾

يَخْرُجُ مِن بَيْنِ الصُّلْبِ وَالتَّرَائِبِ ﴿٧﴾ إِنَّهُ عَلَىٰ رَجْعِهِ

لَقَادِرٌ ﴿٨﴾ يَوْمَ تُبْلَى السَّرَائِرُ ﴿٩﴾ فَمَا لَهُ مِن قُوَّةٍ وَلَا

نَاصِرٍ ﴿١٠﴾ وَالسَّمَاءِ ذَاتِ الرَّجْعِ ﴿١١﴾ وَالْأَرْضِ ذَاتِ

الصَّدْعِ ﴿١٢﴾ إِنَّهُ لَقَوْلٌ فَصْلٌ ﴿١٣﴾ وَمَا هُوَ بِالْهَزْلِ ﴿١٤﴾

إِنَّهُمْ يَكِيدُونَ كَيْدًا ﴿١٥﴾ وَأَكِيدُ كَيْدًا ﴿١٦﴾ فَمَهِّلِ

الْكَافِرِينَ أَمْهِلْهُمْ رُوَيْدًا ﴿١٧﴾

Sūrah 87
al-A 'lā
(The Most High)

This *sūrah* was revealed in Mecca after *sūrah* 81, *al-Takwīr*.
It consists of nineteen verses and may be divided into five parts.

1. The *sūrah* begins with a litany of praise to God who created
all things and formed them well and decreed for every creature
its sustenance and its final destiny (verses 1-5).

2. The Prophet is asked to remind people of God's message,
the Qur'ān, which God has taught him to recite and of which
He has decreed what he should remember and what he should
forget (verses 6-9).

3. Men are declared to be of two kinds: those who fear God
and thus are mindful of His commands and prohibitions, and
those who are negligent, and are here called the most wretched
people. They shall burn in the great Fire in which they shall
neither die and rest, nor live in the true meaning of life (verses
10-13).

4. In contrast, he who purifies himself through alms-giving and
prayers shall indeed be prosperous on the Day of Resurrection.
Yet most men prefer this life to the hereafter, even though the
latter is better and longlasting (verses 14-17).

5. Finally, this truth is declared to have been revealed to Abraham and Moses in the first scrolls or written revelations (verses
18-19).

It is related that the Prophet used to recite this and the following *sūrah* in the *'īd* prayers as well as the Friday prayers if both
fell on the same day. It is further related on the authority of
'Alī that the Prophet especially loved this *sūrah*. It was, moreover, the first *sūrah* to be recited by the Muslim immigrants to
the people of Medina.

In the name of God the All Merciful, the Compassionate

1. Magnify the name of your Lord, the Most High,

2. who created and shaped well,

3. who decreed and guided,*

4. and who brought forth the pasturage,

5. then turned it into blackening drift.

6. We shall teach you to recite and you shall not forget,

7. except what God wills. Surely He knows whatever is uttered aloud and whatever is hidden.*

8. We shall bring you with ease to the lenient way.*

9. Remind, therefore, where the reminder may benefit.

10. He who stands in awe [before God] shall remember.

11. But the most wretched shall evade it.*

12. He who shall burn in the great Fire,

13. in it he shall neither die nor live.

14. Prosperous indeed is he who purifies himself,

(v. 3) i.e., He decreed the sustenance of every creature and guided it to the way of obtaining it, and guided humankind to the way of misery and happiness.

(v. 6-7) These verses relate to the principle of *naskh* (abrogation). What the Prophet was made to forget was what God willed to be abrogated, that is, removed altogether or suppressed.

(v. 8) i.e., the lenient law *(sharī'ah)* of Islām and the performance of righteous deeds.

(v. 11) i.e., Remembrance, which here means the Qur'ān.

(٨٧) سُورَةُ الأَعلى مَكِّيَّةٌ
وَآيَاتُهَا ١٩ نَزَلَتْ بَعْدَ التَّكْوِيرِ

بِسْمِ اللَّهِ الرَّحْمَنِ الرَّحِيمِ

سَبِّحِ اسْمَ رَبِّكَ الأَعْلَى ﴿١﴾ الَّذِى خَلَقَ فَسَوَّى ﴿٢﴾

وَالَّذِى قَدَّرَ فَهَدَى ﴿٣﴾ وَالَّذِى أَخْرَجَ الْمَرْعَى ﴿٤﴾

فَجَعَلَهُ غُثَاءً أَحْوَى ﴿٥﴾ سَنُقْرِئُكَ فَلَا تَنْسَى ﴿٦﴾

إِلَّا مَا شَاءَ اللَّهُ إِنَّهُ يَعْلَمُ الْجَهْرَ وَمَا يَخْفَى ﴿٧﴾ وَنُيَسِّرُكَ

لِلْيُسْرَى ﴿٨﴾ فَذَكِّرْ إِن نَّفَعَتِ الذِّكْرَى ﴿٩﴾ سَيَذَّكَّرُ

مَن يَخْشَى ﴿١٠﴾ وَيَتَجَنَّبُهَا الأَشْقَى ﴿١١﴾ الَّذِى يَصْلَى

النَّارَ الْكُبْرَى ﴿١٢﴾ ثُمَّ لَا يَمُوتُ فِيهَا وَلَا يَحْيَى ﴿١٣﴾

قَدْ أَفْلَحَ مَن تَزَكَّى ﴿١٤﴾ وَذَكَرَ اسْمَ رَبِّهِ فَصَلَّى ﴿١٥﴾

15. mentions the name of his Lord and performs the prayers.*

16. Yet you [humankind] prefer the life of this world,

17. while the life to come is better and more enduring.

18. This is contained in the ancient scrolls,

19. the scrolls of Abraham and Moses.*

(v. 15) According to some commentators, this verse indicates that *zakāt al-fiṭr* (alms of breaking the fast after Ramaḍān) must be given before performing the *'īd* congregational prayers. Others understood the verse in its general sense of giving alms to the poor beggar, if he comes at the time of prayers.

(v. 18-19) This *sūrah,* some of its verses, or verses 33-53 of *Sūrah* 55 are contained in the ancient scrolls revealed to Abraham and Moses.

بَلْ تُؤْثِرُونَ ٱلْحَيَوٰةَ ٱلدُّنْيَا ﴿١٦﴾ وَٱلْأَخِرَةُ خَيْرٌ وَأَبْقَىٰ ﴿١٧﴾

إِنَّ هَٰذَا لَفِى ٱلصُّحُفِ ٱلْأُولَىٰ ﴿١٨﴾ صُحُفِ إِبْرَٰهِيمَ

وَمُوسَىٰ ﴿١٩﴾

Sūrah 88
al-Ghāshīyah
(The Enveloper)

This *sūrah* takes its title from the word *al-ghāshīyah*, which is mentioned in the first verse. The *sūrah* belongs to the middle Meccan period. It consists of twenty-six verses and may be divided into four sections.

1. The *sūrah* begins with a query concerning the Day of Resurrection, which here is called *al-ghāshīyah*, the overwhelming catastrophe which shall envelope all creatures. The event itself is not discussed, but the condition of the people of the Fire is vividly portrayed (verses 1-7).

2. The bliss of the people of Paradise is equally vividly portrayed (v. 8-16).

3. This is followed by calling men to consider God's wisdom in creation. This call is specially addressed to the roaming Bedouins of the desert who are asked to look at the camels and their marvels, the heavens over them, the levelled earth, and the high mountains which serve as landmarks in their travels (verses 17-20).

4. Finally, the *sūrah* concludes with the command to the Prophet to remind people of this Day and of their eventual return to God (verses 21-26).

In the name of God the All Merciful, the Compassionate

1. Has the account of the enveloper come to you,

2. a day on which faces shall be humble,

3. toiling, worn out,*

4. burning in a scorching fire,

5. drinking from a stream of boiling water!

6. They shall have no food except thorny dry cactus,

7. which neither fattens, nor satisfies hunger.*

8. On that day there shall be blissful faces,   .

9. with their labor well-pleased,

10. dwelling in an exalted garden,

11. wherein no idle talk is heard.

12. There is in it a running spring*.

13. In it are couches uplifted,

14. goblets set and ready,

15. cushions arrayed,

16. and colorful carpets spread about.

(v. 3) i.e., having toiled hard in this world, they shall come on the Day of Resurrection worn out with their labor which will profit them nothing.

(v. 6-7) It is related that Ibn 'Abbās interpreted the word *ḍarī'* (thorny cactus) to mean a tree of fire in Hell. According to others, it means stones. The most widely held view, however, is that *ḍarī'* is a cactus plant with sharp thorns and is perhaps poisonous.

(v. 12) This is used to describe the springs of Paradise in general, which are of pure running water.

(٨٨) سُورَةُ الغَاشِيَةِ مَكِّيَّةٌ
وَآيَاتُهَا ٢٦ نَزَلَتْ بَعْدَ الذَّارِيَاتِ

بِسْمِ اللهِ الرَّحْمٰنِ الرَّحِيمِ

هَلْ أَتَاكَ حَدِيثُ الْغَاشِيَةِ ﴿١﴾ وُجُوهٌ يَوْمَئِذٍ خَاشِعَةٌ ﴿٢﴾

عَامِلَةٌ نَّاصِبَةٌ ﴿٣﴾ تَصْلَى نَارًا حَامِيَةً ﴿٤﴾ تُسْقَى مِنْ عَيْنٍ

ءَانِيَةٍ ﴿٥﴾ لَّيْسَ لَهُمْ طَعَامٌ إِلَّا مِن ضَرِيعٍ ﴿٦﴾ لَّا يُسْمِنُ

وَلَا يُغْنِي مِن جُوعٍ ﴿٧﴾ وُجُوهٌ يَوْمَئِذٍ نَّاعِمَةٌ ﴿٨﴾

لِّسَعْيِهَا رَاضِيَةٌ ﴿٩﴾ فِي جَنَّةٍ عَالِيَةٍ ﴿١٠﴾ لَّا تَسْمَعُ فِيهَا

لَاغِيَةً ﴿١١﴾ فِيهَا عَيْنٌ جَارِيَةٌ ﴿١٢﴾ فِيهَا سُرُرٌ مَّرْفُوعَةٌ ﴿١٣﴾

وَأَكْوَابٌ مَّوْضُوعَةٌ ﴿١٤﴾ وَنَمَارِقُ مَصْفُوفَةٌ ﴿١٥﴾ وَزَرَابِيُّ

مَبْثُوثَةٌ ﴿١٦﴾ أَفَلَا يَنظُرُونَ إِلَى الْإِبِلِ كَيْفَ خُلِقَتْ ﴿١٧﴾

17. Do they not look at the camels, how they were created;

18. at the heaven, how it was lifted up;

19. at the mountains, how they were erected;

20. and the earth, how it was levelled!

21. Remind therefore, for you are only one who reminds;

22. you are not set in authority over them.

23. But as for him who turns away and rejects faith,

24. God shall punish him with a most terrible torment.

25. Surely to Us shall be their return,

26. and with Us shall be their final reckoning.

وَإِلَى ٱلسَّمَآءِ كَيْفَ رُفِعَتْ ﴿١٨﴾ وَإِلَى ٱلْجِبَالِ كَيْفَ

نُصِبَتْ ﴿١٩﴾ وَإِلَى ٱلْأَرْضِ كَيْفَ سُطِحَتْ ﴿٢٠﴾ فَذَكِّرْ

إِنَّمَآ أَنتَ مُذَكِّرٌ ﴿٢١﴾ لَّسْتَ عَلَيْهِم بِمُصَيْطِرٍ ﴿٢٢﴾ إِلَّا

مَن تَوَلَّىٰ وَكَفَرَ ﴿٢٣﴾ فَيُعَذِّبُهُ ٱللَّهُ ٱلْعَذَابَ ٱلْأَكْبَرَ ﴿٢٤﴾

إِنَّ إِلَيْنَآ إِيَابَهُمْ ﴿٢٥﴾ ثُمَّ إِنَّ عَلَيْنَا حِسَابَهُم ﴿٢٦﴾

Sūrah 89
al-Fajr
(The Dawn)

This *sūrah* was revealed in Mecca after *sūrah* 92, *al-Layl*. It consists of thirty verses and may be divided into five sections.

1. The *sūrah* begins with an oath offered as a challenge to those possessed of a prudent mind (verses 1-5).

2. This is followed by citing an example of ancient communities. 'ĀD, Thamūd, and Pharaoh and his people, who were all wiped out in punishment for their wickedness (verses 6-14).

3. This is followed by the reminder that people must not only accept God's favors, but also afflictions as a trial of faith. People are reminded that they also must care for the orphan, feed the poor and not devour the inheritance of the weak (verses 16-20).

4. A further reminder follows of the Day of Resurrection and its great cataclysmic events. The wicked shall then be filled with remorse, but remorse shall avail them nothing (verses 21-26).

5. The *sūrah* ends with a moving consolation for the soul at peace with God which shall be summoned to everlasting bliss in Paradise in the company of God's faithful servants (verses 27-30).

In the name of God the All Merciful, the Compassionate

1. By the dawn,

2. and the ten nights!

3. By the even and the odd,

4. and the night when it passes on:

5. Is there in this an oath for one possessed of a prudent mind?*

(v. 1-5) Commentators have widely differed with regard to the meanings of each of the oaths in the first three verses. Thus dawn is said to refer either to dawn as such, to the morning of the feast of sacrifice *('id al-adha)*, it being the last of the ten nights here mentioned, or even to the entire day. As for the ten nights, they were said to refer either to the first ten days of Dhū al-Hijjah (the pilgrimage month and the last month of the Muslim calendar), the first ten days of Muharram (the first month of the year), or, finally, the first ten days of Ramadan. The first view, however, is the one most widely accepted by classical commentators.

With regard to the even and the odd (*al-shaf', al-watr)*, the latter is said to be the last day of the pilgrimage ritual, the day of 'Arafāh, and the former the day of sacrifice, following the ten nights already mentioned. This is to say *al-watr* is the ninth, an odd number, and *al-shaf'*, the tenth, an even number.

A second view refers *al-shaf'* and *al-watr* to the two days following the day of sacrifice. A third view is that the even and the odd here refer to the entire creation. According to a fourth view, they refer to the noon and evening prayers. According to yet another view, God is the odd, being One, and the male and female of His creatures are the even.

More recent commentators have offered an entirely different interpretation. They say Dawn is the time when daylight breaks forth ... the ten nights are the ten nights resembling dawn. This is because during them, the light of the moon dispels darkness but the light in the end is overcome by it. These ten nights are not specified in every month because the light of the moon may appear on the first night of the lunar month. It may also be too weak on that night to be considered light in the proper sense of the word. Thus the ten nights may begin either on the first or second night of the lunar month. The even and the odd are the even and odd of these nights. God swore by these nights together, then by the even and odd of their numbers. After swearing by the different stages of light, God swore by night as such, intending by it darkness.

(٨٩) سُورَةُ الفَجرِ مَكِّيَّة
وَآياتُها ٣٠ نَزَلَت بَعدَ اللَّيلِ

بِسمِ اللهِ الرَّحمنِ الرَّحيمِ

وَالفَجرِ ﴿١﴾ وَلَيالٍ عَشرٍ ﴿٢﴾ وَالشَّفعِ وَالوَترِ ﴿٣﴾
وَاللَّيلِ إِذا يَسرِ ﴿٤﴾ هَل في ذلِكَ قَسَمٌ لِذي حِجرٍ ﴿٥﴾

6. Have you not considered how your Lord dealt with 'Ād —

7. Iram with their pillars—

8. the like of whom were not created in the lands?*

9. And with Thamūd who hollowed rocks in the valley;*

10. and Pharaoh with his pegs?

11. They all acted wickedly in the land;

12. therein they spread much corruption.

13. Thus your Lord sent down upon them a scourge of torment,

14. for your Lord is surely on watch.

According to other commentators it is perhaps best not to identify the ten nights but only observe that they are of special significance, which God alone knows. The even and odd reflect the spirit of prayer and may refer to specific prayers as indicated in a *ḥadīth* tradition.

(v. 6-8) 'Ād was an ancient tribe whose ancestor was 'Ād, son of Iram. God sent to them the prophet Hūd whom they rejected, and thus they were destroyed (Q. 7: 65-72). The pillars are pillars which they used to hold up their tents.

(v. 9) Thamūd were another Arab tribe which may have lived in the desert between Arabia and Syria or in Wādī al-Qura near Mecca. God sent to them the prophet Ṣāliḥ whom they rejected (see below, *sūrah* 95). They were also destroyed as punishment for their rejection of faith in God and His prophet.

(v. 10) Some classical commentators have held several views concerning Pharaoh's pegs. The first is that Pharaoh fixed four strong pegs in the ground across which he laid his wife, and placed a heavy millstone on her back, which crushed her to death. This he did because she had accepted faith in God and cared for the prophet Moses.

Later commentators considered the pegs here to mean "massive and strong edifices".

Even more specifically some have taken the pegs here to refer to the Pyramids of ancient Egypt.

أَلَمْ تَرَ كَيْفَ فَعَلَ رَبُّكَ بِعَادٍ ﴿٦﴾ إِرَمَ ذَاتِ ٱلْعِمَادِ ﴿٧﴾

ٱلَّتِي لَمْ يُخْلَقْ مِثْلُهَا فِي ٱلْبِلَٰدِ ﴿٨﴾ وَثَمُودَ ٱلَّذِينَ جَابُوا۟

ٱلصَّخْرَ بِٱلْوَادِ ﴿٩﴾ وَفِرْعَوْنَ ذِي ٱلْأَوْتَادِ ﴿١٠﴾ ٱلَّذِينَ

طَغَوْا۟ فِي ٱلْبِلَٰدِ ﴿١١﴾ فَأَكْثَرُوا۟ فِيهَا ٱلْفَسَادَ ﴿١٢﴾

فَصَبَّ عَلَيْهِمْ رَبُّكَ سَوْطَ عَذَابٍ ﴿١٣﴾ إِنَّ رَبَّكَ

لَبِٱلْمِرْصَادِ ﴿١٤﴾ فَأَمَّا ٱلْإِنسَٰنُ إِذَا مَا ٱبْتَلَٰهُ رَبُّهُ

15. Yet as for man, when his Lord tests him by honoring and blessing him with comfort, he says, "My Lord has honored me."

16. But when He tries him by diminishing the measure of his provisions, he says, "My Lord has despised me."

17. No, indeed, but you do not honor the orphan

18. nor do you urge one another to feed the needy.

19. Rather, you devour the inheritance [of the orphan] unsparingly,

20. and you love wealth with an exceeding love.

21. No, indeed, when the earth shall be levelled, devastated,

22. and your Lord comes with the angels rank upon rank;

23. when on that day Hell shall be brought forth: on that day man will remember, but how will the remembrance benefit him!

24. Then he shall say, "Would that I had forwarded [some good] for my life!"

25. For on that day no one shall punish the like of His punishment,

26. nor will anyone bind in fetters like His fetters.

27. O soul at peace,

28. return to your Lord content and He pleased with you.

29. Enter into the company of my servants.

30. Enter into My Paradise!

فَأَكْرَمَهُ وَنَعَّمَهُ فَيَقُولُ رَبِّي أَكْرَمَنِ ﴿١٥﴾ وَأَمَّا إِذَا

مَا ابْتَلَاهُ فَقَدَرَ عَلَيْهِ رِزْقَهُ فَيَقُولُ رَبِّي أَهَانَنِ ﴿١٦﴾

كَلَّا بَل لَّا تُكْرِمُونَ الْيَتِيمَ ﴿١٧﴾ وَلَا تَحَاضُّونَ عَلَى

طَعَامِ الْمِسْكِينِ ﴿١٨﴾ وَتَأْكُلُونَ التُّرَاثَ أَكْلًا لَّمًّا ﴿١٩﴾

وَتُحِبُّونَ الْمَالَ حُبًّا جَمًّا ﴿٢٠﴾ كَلَّا إِذَا دُكَّتِ الْأَرْضُ

دَكًّا دَكًّا ﴿٢١﴾ وَجَاءَ رَبُّكَ وَالْمَلَكُ صَفًّا صَفًّا ﴿٢٢﴾

وَجِائِءَ يَوْمَئِذٍ بِجَهَنَّمَ يَوْمَئِذٍ يَتَذَكَّرُ الْإِنسَانُ وَأَنَّى

لَهُ الذِّكْرَىٰ ﴿٢٣﴾ يَقُولُ يَا لَيْتَنِي قَدَّمْتُ لِحَيَاتِي

فَيَوْمَئِذٍ لَّا يُعَذِّبُ عَذَابَهُ أَحَدٌ ﴿٢٥﴾ وَلَا يُوثِقُ وَثَاقَهُ

أَحَدٌ ﴿٢٦﴾ يَا أَيَّتُهَا النَّفْسُ الْمُطْمَئِنَّةُ ﴿٢٧﴾ ارْجِعِي إِلَىٰ

رَبِّكِ رَاضِيَةً مَّرْضِيَّةً ﴿٢٨﴾ فَادْخُلِي فِي عِبَادِي ﴿٢٩﴾

وَادْخُلِي جَنَّتِي ﴿٣٠﴾

Sūrah 90
al-Balad
(The Town)

This *sūrah* was revealed in Mecca at an uncertain date. It consists of twenty verses and deals with the following themes:

1. The *sūrah* opens with a series of oaths followed by the assertion that man was created to endure the hardships of life (verses 1-4).

2. The *sūrah* goes on to reproach man for his arrogance and to remind him that God gave him faculties of sight and speech and a mind to distinguish the ways of good and evil (verses 5-10).

3. In return for God's favors, man is enjoined to show mercy to the hungry, the orphan, the destitute and the captive (verses 11-16). Buying the freedom of captives from slavery is, according to the Qur'ān, one of the greatest of good deeds.

4. The *sūrah* concludes by contrasting the people of the right hand, the people of faith, with the people of the left hand, the rejectors of faith (verses 17-20).

In the name of God the All Merciful, the Compassionate

1. No, but I swear by this town [Mecca],

2. while you [Muhammad] dwell in this town;*

3. by him who begot and him who was begotten,*

4. indeed we created man to endure hardship.*

5. Does he then think that no one shall have power over him?

6. He says, "I have consumed abundant wealth!"

7. Does he reckon that no one sees him?

8. Have we not given him two eyes,

9. a tongue and two lips,

10. and guided him to the two highways?

11. Yet he has not assaulted the steep road.*

12. Would that you knew what the steep road is!

(v. 1-2) The word *hullun* (dwelling) has also been interpreted to mean that it was lawful *(halāl)* for the Prophet to dwell in Mecca or to fight in its sacred environs, while it is not lawful for any other man to do so until the Day of Resurrection.

(v. 3) According to classical commentators, the begetter is Adam and the begotten are his children. Some have interpreted this verse to refer to Abraham and his descendents who dwelt in Mecca. Others have interpreted this verse to refer to all beings subject to the law of generation, including humans and animals.

(v. 4) Some classical commentators interpreted this verse to mean that "He created man with a good and strong stature".

(v. 11) The word *'aqabah* (steep road) has been interpreted by some classical commentators concretely to mean a mountain in Hell or various stations in Hell. Another more widely accepted view is that *al-'aqabah* is the way of the good which if traversed by man will lead him to salvation from the Fire.

(٩٠) سُورَةُ الْبَلَدِ مَكِّيَّةٌ
وَآيَاتُهَا ٢٠ نَزَلَتْ بَعْدَ ق

بِسْمِ اللهِ الرَّحْمَنِ الرَّحِيمِ

لَا أُقْسِمُ بِهَذَا الْبَلَدِ ﴿١﴾ وَأَنْتَ حِلٌّ بِهَذَا الْبَلَدِ ﴿٢﴾

وَوَالِدٍ وَمَا وَلَدَ ﴿٣﴾ لَقَدْ خَلَقْنَا الْإِنْسَانَ فِي كَبَدٍ ﴿٤﴾

أَيَحْسَبُ أَنْ لَّنْ يَقْدِرَ عَلَيْهِ أَحَدٌ ﴿٥﴾ يَقُولُ أَهْلَكْتُ مَالًا

لُّبَدًا ﴿٦﴾ أَيَحْسَبُ أَنْ لَّمْ يَرَهُ أَحَدٌ ﴿٧﴾ أَلَمْ نَجْعَلْ لَّهُ

عَيْنَيْنِ ﴿٨﴾ وَلِسَانًا وَشَفَتَيْنِ ﴿٩﴾ وَهَدَيْنَاهُ النَّجْدَيْنِ ﴿١٠﴾

فَلَا اقْتَحَمَ الْعَقَبَةَ ﴿١١﴾ وَمَا أَدْرَاكَ مَا الْعَقَبَةُ ﴿١٢﴾

13. It is the freeing of a captive,

14. or giving food on a day of famine—

15. to an orphan, next-of-kin,

16. or to a needy man in destitution.

17. And also that he be one of the people of faith who enjoin one another in steadfastness and mercy.

18. These shall be the people of the right hand!

19. But those who rejected our signs shall be the people of the left hand.*

20. They shall dwell in a Fire closed over them.

(v. 19) On the Day of Resurrection when people shall be given their book of deeds in their right or left hand (see above, *sūrah* 84).

فَكُّ رَقَبَةٍ ﴿١٣﴾ أَوْ إِطْعَامٌ فِى يَوْمٍ ذِى مَسْغَبَةٍ ﴿١٤﴾

يَتِيمًا ذَا مَقْرَبَةٍ ﴿١٥﴾ أَوْ مِسْكِينًا ذَا مَتْرَبَةٍ ﴿١٦﴾ ثُمَّ كَانَ مِنَ

ٱلَّذِينَ ءَامَنُوا۟ وَتَوَاصَوْا۟ بِٱلصَّبْرِ وَتَوَاصَوْا۟ بِٱلْمَرْحَمَةِ ﴿١٧﴾

أُو۟لَٰٓئِكَ أَصْحَٰبُ ٱلْمَيْمَنَةِ ﴿١٨﴾ وَٱلَّذِينَ كَفَرُوا۟ بِـَٔايَٰتِنَا

هُمْ أَصْحَٰبُ ٱلْمَشْـَٔمَةِ ﴿١٩﴾ عَلَيْهِمْ نَارٌ مُّؤْصَدَةٌ ﴿٢٠﴾

Sūrah 91
al-Shams
(The Sun)

This *sūrah* was revealed in Mecca after *sūrah* 97, *al-Qadr*.
It consists of fifteen verses and may be divided into three parts.

1. The *sūrah* opens with a series of oaths by heavenly bodies,
the phenomena of nature, the human soul and God, who created
all things (verses 1-8).

2. The soul is declared to be endowed by God with the rational
capacity to choose wickedness or piety. Hence, the surah goes
on to assert that he who purifies his soul does well, but he who
corrupts it shall indeed fail (verses 9-10).

3. The *sūrah* concludes with the example of the ancient tribe
of Thamūd who chose error instead of guidance. God destroyed
them utterly for their rejection of God's command (verses 11-
15).

In the name of God the All Merciful, the Compassionate

1. By the sun and its morning brightness,

2. and the moon when it follows it!

3. By the day when it displays it,

4. and the night when it covers it!*

5. By the heaven and He who built it,

6. and the earth and He who spread it!

7. By the soul and He who formed it,

8. then inspired it with its wickedness and righteousness!

9. He has indeed prospered who purifies it,

10. and has failed, he who corrupts it.*

11. Thamūd cried lies in their insolence,

12. when the most wretched of them rose up.*

(v. 3-4) Some commentators have identified the object of the verbs "to display" and "to cover" as the earth. Thus they read verse 3 as "By the day when it adorns the earth" and verse 4 "and the night when it covers the earth".

(v. 9-10) Some commentators have identified the subject in verses 9-10 as God. They thus read verse 9 as "He whose soul God purifies has indeed prospered" and verse 10 as "and he whose soul God corrupts, that soul has indeed failed".

(v. 11-12) This is a reference to Qūdar b. Sālif who killed the she-camel of the prophet Ṣāliḥ. The man was known in tradition as "the little redhead (uḥaymar) of Thamūd." (Cf. Sūrah 54:23-32).

(٩١) سُورَةُ الشَّمْسِ مَكِّيَّة
وَآيَاتُهَا ١٥ نَزَلَتْ بَعْدَ الْقَدْرِ

بِسْمِ اللهِ الرَّحْمَنِ الرَّحِيمِ

وَالشَّمْسِ وَضُحَاهَا ۝ وَالْقَمَرِ إِذَا تَلَاهَا ۝ وَالنَّهَارِ إِذَا جَلَّاهَا ۝ وَالَّيْلِ إِذَا يَغْشَاهَا ۝ وَالسَّمَاءِ وَمَا بَنَاهَا ۝ وَالْأَرْضِ وَمَا طَحَاهَا ۝ وَنَفْسٍ وَمَا سَوَّاهَا ۝ فَأَلْهَمَهَا فُجُورَهَا وَتَقْوَاهَا ۝ قَدْ أَفْلَحَ مَن زَكَّاهَا ۝ وَقَدْ خَابَ مَن دَسَّاهَا ۝ كَذَّبَتْ ثَمُودُ بِطَغْوَاهَا ۝ إِذِ انْبَعَثَ أَشْقَاهَا ۝ فَقَالَ لَهُمْ

13. Then the apostle of God (Ṣāliḥ) said to them,
    "Beward the she-camel of God that you harm
    her when she drinks!"*

14. But they gave the lie to him and slew her.* Thus
    their Lord crushed them for their sin, inflicting
    equal punishment on each of them.

15. Nor did He fear its consequences!*

(v. 13) The she-camel of the prophet Ṣāliḥ was his miracle which God
brought forth from a rock. The prophet Ṣāliḥ agreed with the people
that one day they and their animals would drink at the water and the
next day only the she-camel would drink. The people, however, all agreed
to slay the she-camel and when they did so, God became wrathful with
them and destroyed them.

(v. 14) The verb 'aqara means to hamstring or wound. Most commentators have, however, interpreted it here to mean to kill.

(v. 15) In another reading, "he" refers not to God, but to the man
who slew the she-camel and did not fear the consequence of his deed.
The most widely accepted view, however, based on the official reading,
refers the verb to God, as in the previous verse.

رَسُولُ اللهِ نَاقَةَ اللهِ وَسُقْيَٰهَا ۞ فَكَذَّبُوهُ فَعَقَرُوهَا

فَدَمْدَمَ عَلَيْهِمْ رَبُّهُمْ بِذَنبِهِمْ فَسَوَّىٰهَا ۞ وَلَا يَخَافُ

عُقْبَٰهَا ۞

Sūrah 92
al-Layl
(The Night)

This *sūrah* was revealed in Mecca after *sūrah* 87, *āl-A'la*. It consists of twenty-one verses and deals with the following themes:

1. The *sūrah* begins with the oath by the night and day, and by Him who created the male and the female. This is followed by the assertion that the works of humankind have diverse ends (verses 1-4).

2. This assertion is then explained by distinguishing the person of good deeds, who gives alms and assents to the good and the true, from him who is miserly and rejects the truth. The former shall be assisted in his striving for the good, and the latter in his striving for even greater evil (verses 5-11).

3. This is followed by warning of the torment of the wicked and promise of rich reward for the righteous. Guidance in the end comes from God, in whose hands are the affairs of this world and the next (verses 12-20).

In the name of God the All Merciful, the Compassionate

1. By the night when it envelopes,

2. and the day when it shines in splendor!

3. By Him who created the male and the female:

4. your striving is surely to diverse ends.

5. As for him who gives [alms], fears God,

6. and confirms virtue,

7. We shall surely render easy his way to the good.

8. But as for him who is miserly and self-sufficient,

9. and who gives the lie to virtue,

10. We shall surely render easy his way to hardship.*

11. Nor will his wealth profit him anything when he perishes.

12. Surely with Us rests guidance,

13. and to Us belong the hereafter and this world.

14. Thus have I warned you of a Fire blazing!

15. None shall burn in it but the most miserable,

16. he who cries lies and turns away.

17. Yet the most God-fearing shall be removed from it,

18. he who spends of his wealth in alms to purify himself,

19. obliged to no one for a favor to be recompensed,

20. but only seeking the face of his Lord Most High.

21. He shall surely be satisfied.

(v. 10) i.e., the way to evil.

(٩٢) سُورَةُ الليلِ مَكِّيَّة
وَآيَاتُهَا ٢١ نَزَلَتْ بَعْدَ الأعْلَى

بِسْمِ اللهِ الرَّحْمٰنِ الرَّحِيمِ

وَالَّيْلِ إِذَا يَغْشَىٰ ﴿١﴾ وَالنَّهَارِ إِذَا تَجَلَّىٰ ﴿٢﴾ وَمَا خَلَقَ الذَّكَرَ وَالْأُنثَىٰ ﴿٣﴾ إِنَّ سَعْيَكُمْ لَشَتَّىٰ ﴿٤﴾ فَأَمَّا مَنْ أَعْطَىٰ وَاتَّقَىٰ ﴿٥﴾ وَصَدَّقَ بِالْحُسْنَىٰ ﴿٦﴾ فَسَنُيَسِّرُهُ لِلْيُسْرَىٰ ﴿٧﴾ وَأَمَّا مَن بَخِلَ وَاسْتَغْنَىٰ ﴿٨﴾ وَكَذَّبَ بِالْحُسْنَىٰ ﴿٩﴾ فَسَنُيَسِّرُهُ لِلْعُسْرَىٰ ﴿١٠﴾ وَمَا يُغْنِي عَنْهُ مَالُهُ إِذَا تَرَدَّىٰ ﴿١١﴾ إِنَّ عَلَيْنَا لَلْهُدَىٰ ﴿١٢﴾ وَإِنَّ لَنَا لَلْآخِرَةَ وَالْأُولَىٰ ﴿١٣﴾ فَأَنذَرْتُكُمْ نَارًا تَلَظَّىٰ ﴿١٤﴾ لَا يَصْلَاهَا إِلَّا الْأَشْقَى ﴿١٥﴾ الَّذِي كَذَّبَ وَتَوَلَّىٰ ﴿١٦﴾

وَسَيُجَنَّبُهَا ٱلْأَتْقَى ﴿١٧﴾ ٱلَّذِى يُؤْتِى مَالَهُۥ يَتَزَكَّىٰ ﴿١٨﴾

وَمَا لِأَحَدٍ عِندَهُۥ مِن نِّعْمَةٍ تُجْزَىٰٓ ﴿١٩﴾ إِلَّا ٱبْتِغَآءَ وَجْهِ

رَبِّهِ ٱلْأَعْلَىٰ ﴿٢٠﴾ وَلَسَوْفَ يَرْضَىٰ ﴿٢١﴾

Sūrah 93
al-Ḍuḥā
(The Bright Forenoon)

The present *sūrah* was revealed in Mecca after *sūrah* 89, *al-Fajr*. It consists of eleven verses. It is related on the authority of Ubayy b. Ka'b (a well-known Companion and one of the chief authorities on Qur'ānic interpretation and recitation) that the Prophet commanded him to pronounce a *takbīr* ("God is most great") when reciting this *sūrah*. Commentators have, however, differed as to when and how the *takbīr* is to be pronounced. According to some, it is to be uttered before the *sūrah*, and according to others at its end. As for the words of the *takbīr*, some have said that the reciter should proclaim, *"Allāhu akbar"* (God is most great), only. Others said that he should proclaim, "God is most great, there is no god but God, God is most great." The reason for this *takbīr* is that revelation to the Prophet was interrupted for some time. But when Gabriel finally came to him and revealed this entire *sūrah*, the Prophet cried out joyfully, "Allāhu akbar!"

The *sūrah* deals with the following themes:

1. It opens with an oath followed by the consoling assertion to the Prophet that God has not abandoned or despised him (verses 1-5).

2. The Prophet is further reminded of God's favor towards him (verses 6-8).

3. In return for God's favor and acts of mercy, the Prophet is enjoined to show kindness to the orphan and the needy, and to proclaim to others the bounty of his Lord (verses 9-11).

In the name of God the All Merciful, the Compassionate

1. By the bright forenoon,

2. and the night when it is still:

3. your Lord has neither forsaken you nor despised you.*

4. Surely the hereafter is better for you than this world;

5. and your Lord shall surely give you, and you will be satisfied.

6. Did He not find you, an orphan, and shelter you?

7. Did He not find you erring and guide you?*

8. Did He not find you needy* and provide for you?

9. As for the orphan, do not oppress him;

10. as for the beggar, do not scold him;

11. and as for the bounty of your Lord, proclaim it.

(v. 1-3) It is related by many early authorities that the Prophet was ill for several days, unable to rise up in prayer or receive revelation. It is said that a woman, perhaps the wife of his wicked uncle, Abū Lahab (see below, *sūrah* 111), said to him, "O Muhammad, it seems to me that your Satan has abandoned you." According to other reports, he was taunted with these or similar words by the Meccan Associators. Others said that his wife Khadījah said to him with manifest sadness for his troubled state, "It seems to me that your Lord has come to despise you." Thus the *sūrah* was sent down to reassure the Prophet of God's favor towards him.

(v. 7) According to some commentators, this verse means that the Prophet had strayed from Divine precepts (*sharī'a*), not the basic faith in the Oneness *(tawḥīd)* of God. According to others, this simply referred to the time when the Prophet was once lost in the alleys of Mecca and God sent Gabriel to show him the way. Still others asserted that this verse refers to the time when the Prophet was on a journey with his uncle Abū Ṭālib. As they journeyed by night, the prophet's mount strayed away from the road and Gabriel came and set it back on the right course. The first view, however, is the most plausible and widely accepted interpretation and is supported by the Qur'ān itself in many places.

(v. 8) i.e., burdened with family cares.

(٩٣) سُورَةُ الضُّحَى مَكِّيَّة وَآيَاتُهَا ١١ نَزَلَتْ بَعْدَ الفَجْرِ

بِسْمِ اللهِ الرَّحْمٰنِ الرَّحِيمِ

وَالضُّحَى ﴿١﴾ وَالَّيْلِ إِذَا سَجَى ﴿٢﴾ مَا وَدَّعَكَ رَبُّكَ وَمَا قَلَى ﴿٣﴾ وَلَلْآخِرَةُ خَيْرٌ لَّكَ مِنَ الْأُولَى ﴿٤﴾ وَلَسَوْفَ يُعْطِيكَ رَبُّكَ فَتَرْضَى ﴿٥﴾ أَلَمْ يَجِدْكَ يَتِيمًا فَآوَى ﴿٦﴾ وَوَجَدَكَ ضَالًّا فَهَدَى ﴿٧﴾ وَوَجَدَكَ عَائِلًا فَأَغْنَى ﴿٨﴾ فَأَمَّا الْيَتِيمَ فَلَا تَقْهَرْ ﴿٩﴾ وَأَمَّا السَّائِلَ فَلَا تَنْهَرْ ﴿١٠﴾ وَأَمَّا بِنِعْمَةِ رَبِّكَ فَحَدِّثْ ﴿١١﴾

Sūrah 94
al-Inshirāh
(Relief)

This *sūrah* was revealed in Mecca after the previous one. Some early authorities in fact considered the two *sūrahs* as one. They thus recited them in one *rak'ah* (unit) of the prayers and did not separate them with the invocation, "In the name of God the All Merciful, the Compassionate".

The *sūrah* consists of eight verses and continues the main thought of the one before it. Its major themes are:

1. God reminds the Prophet of His favor towards Him (verses 1-4).

2. The Prophet is further reassured, and through him all men, that with every hardship comes ease. This is repeated twice for emphasis (verses 5-6).

3. Finally the Prophet is commanded to turn to God in prayer after he has ended the toils of the day (verses 7-8).

In the name of God the All Merciful, the Compassionate

1. Have we not relieved your breast for you,*

2. and removed from you your burden

3. which had weighed so heavily upon your back,

4. and exalted high your fame?*

5. Surely with every hardship comes ease!

6. Surely with every hardship comes ease!

7. So when you are free [from daily cares], exert yourself [in prayers],

8. and to your Lord turn your desire.

(v. 1) Commentators have differed in their interpretation of this verse. According to some, relief came to the Prophet with the coming of revelation after his period of solitude on Mount Ḥirā'. According to others, the reference here is to the end of the interruption (*fatrah*) of revelation which occurred at the beginning of Muhammad's prophetic career. Other commentators took the word *nashraḥ* (we open up) literally, to mean an opening up of the Prophet's breast. The following story was related on the authority of Abū Hurayrah.

When the Prophet was yet a youth tending sheep in the desert, two angels came to him in human form. They laid him gently on the ground and opened up his breast. They then took out of his heart something like a dark blood clot which signified malice and envy and put in its place mercy and compassion. Then they closed up his breast without his feeling any pain or fatigue. Having released him, they commanded him to show mercy to all people, young and old.

(v. 4) i.e., through the *shahādah* (the witness of faith), in which the Prophet's name is coupled with that of God in the proclamation, "I bear witness that there is no god but God and that Muhammad is the apostle of God".

(v. 5-6) The word *'usr* (hardship) is used in both verses with the definite article indicating singularity, while the word *yusr* is used indefinitely throughout to indicate plurality. It is reported that the Prophet therefore said, "One hardship can never overcome two *yusrs* [instances of relief or ease]." He also said, "Even if hardship were to enter a stone, ease would pursue it and drive it out".

(٩٤) سُورَةُ الشَّرْحِ مَكِّيَّةٌ
وَآيَاتُهَا ٨ نَزَلَتْ بَعْدَ الضُّحَى

بِسْمِ اللهِ الرَّحْمَنِ الرَّحِيمِ

أَلَمْ نَشْرَحْ لَكَ صَدْرَكَ ﴿١﴾ وَوَضَعْنَا عَنكَ وِزْرَكَ ﴿٢﴾

الَّذِى أَنقَضَ ظَهْرَكَ ﴿٣﴾ وَرَفَعْنَا لَكَ ذِكْرَكَ ﴿٤﴾

فَإِنَّ مَعَ الْعُسْرِ يُسْرًا ﴿٥﴾ إِنَّ مَعَ الْعُسْرِ يُسْرًا ﴿٦﴾

فَإِذَا فَرَغْتَ فَانصَبْ ﴿٧﴾ وَإِلَى رَبِّكَ فَارْغَب ﴿٨﴾

103

Sūrah 95
al-Tīn
(The Fig)

This *sūrah* was revealed in Mecca after *sūrah* 85, *al-Burūj*. The *sūrah* takes its title from the first word, *al-Tīn*. Since most commentators interpret the fig and olive mentioned in this *sūrah* to refer to specific places or epochs, it is more appropriate to render it "fig", rather than "fig tree", which may be misleading.

The *sūrah* consists of eight verses and deals with two major themes.

1. It opens with a series of oaths which relate symbolically to human civilization through the fig and olive tree, which signify agricultural life. The oaths further relate, through the reference to Mt. Sinai and Mecca, the two locii of Divine revelation to man's spiritual history (verses 1-3).

2. This is followed by the assertion that man may be of either the best stature, physically and spiritually, or may sink to the lowest condition (verses 4-5). The three remaining verses (verses 6-8) are further elaborations on this theme.

In the name of God the All Merciful, the Compassionate

1. By the fig and the olive!

2. By Mount Sinai,

3. and this town secure:*

(v. 1-3) Commentators have widely differed as to what the fig and the olive refer to. According to some, the fig is the mosque of Damascus. Others said that it is a mountain near Damascus. A third view is that it is the place of worship of the people of the cave (see *sūrah* 18). A fourth view is that it is the place of worship of the prophet Noah which is on the Jūdī (Mt. Ararāt). As for the olive, it is, according to some early authorities, Jerusalem. Others interpreted both the fig and the olive to refer to figs and olives in the general sense. It is generally agreed that Ţūr Sīnīn (Mt. Sinai) is the mountain on which God spoke to Moses. The secure town is Mecca. Some later commentators regarded these as three places in which God sent great prophets with major revelations. The first is the place of the fig and olive, that is, Jerusalem, where Jesus was sent. The second was Mt. Sinai where God sent Moses, and the third is Mecca where Muḥammad was sent.

However, the modern rationalistic school of the 19th and early 20th century held that the fig here is intended to represent the first period of humanity when man clothed himself with fig leaves and when Adam dwelt in Paradise. The olive refers to the time of Noah and his children when he sent the dove out of the ark and it returned to him with the olive branch. Thus he was glad with the knowledge that the waters of the deluge no longer covered the earth. According to this view Ţūr Sīnīn is Mt. Sinai and the secure town is Mecca, which God honored with the Kaaba.

Some modern commentators assert that it may be observed that while the olive is mentioned several times in the Qur'ān the fig is mentioned only once in this *sūrah*. It must further be concluded that nothing can be said with certainty concerning this matter. All that we can say is that the mention of the fig and olive here may refer to places or memories having some relationship to religion and faith, or some relationship to man when he was created in the best of stature. This may have been in the Garden of Paradise in which man began his life. In this way this allusion would fit well with the reality which is presented in this *sūrah*, in accordance with the general approach of the Qur'ān.

(٩٥) سُورَةِ التِّينِ مَكِّيَّة
وَآيَاتُهَا ٨ نَزَلَتْ بَعْدَ الْبُرُوجِ

بِسْمِ اللهِ الرَّحْمَنِ الرَّحِيمِ

وَالتِّينِ وَالزَّيْتُونِ ﴿١﴾ وَطُورِ سِينِينَ ﴿٢﴾ وَهَذَا
الْبَلَدِ الْأَمِينِ ﴿٣﴾ لَقَدْ خَلَقْنَا الْإِنسَانَ فِي أَحْسَنِ

4. We have indeed created man in the best of stature.

5. Then We returned him to the lowest of the low.

6. Except those who have faith and perform good deeds: they shall have an unfailing reward.

7. What then shall make you [man] give the lie to the last judgment?

8. Is not God the most just of all judges?

تَقْوِيمٍ ۝ ثُمَّ رَدَدْنَٰهُ أَسْفَلَ سَٰفِلِينَ ۝ إِلَّا ٱلَّذِينَ

ءَامَنُوا۟ وَعَمِلُوا۟ ٱلصَّٰلِحَٰتِ فَلَهُمْ أَجْرٌ غَيْرُ مَمْنُونٍ ۝

فَمَا يُكَذِّبُكَ بَعْدُ بِٱلدِّينِ ۝ أَلَيْسَ ٱللَّهُ بِأَحْكَمِ

ٱلْحَٰكِمِينَ ۝

Sūrah 96
al-'Alaq
(The Blood Clot)

This *sūrah* consists of nineteen verses, the first five of which were the first revelation of the Qur'ān. The rest of the *sūrah*, as may be seen from the context, was revealed later when the Prophet had already begun to preach the new faith. The major themes of this surah are the following:

1. The Qur'ān begins through the opening verses of this *sūrah* with the command to the Prophet to recite in the name of God, whose power and magnanimity are here related to the gift of revelation to man (verses 1-5).

2. Man is declared to be arrogant in his feeling of self-sufficiency. Yet to God shall all things return (verses 6-8).

3. A new theme is here introduced in that the text seems to refer to a sepcific man who had thought to prevent the Prophet from praying in the precincts of the Kaaba (verses 9-14). These verses, however, could apply to any similar situation at any time.

4. This admonition is then followed by a stern threat of Divine punishment in the Fire. The *sūrah* ends with a consoling call to the Prophet to draw near to God and bow down in prayer before Him (verses 15-19).

In the name of God the All Merciful, the Compassionate

1. Recite in the name of your Lord who created,

2. created man from a blood clot.

3. Recite, for your Lord is most magnanimous—

4. Who taught by the pen;

5. taught man that which he did not know.*

(v. 1-5) These five verses are generally believed to have been the first utterances to be revealed of the Qur'ān. It is related on the authority of 'A'ishah and other *hadīth* transmittors that the Prophet used to go in retreat to a cave on Mt. Hirā' near Mecca where he spent many nights in contemplation. This he did until suddenly an angel, later identified as Gabriel, came to him saying, "Recite!" He answered, "I cannot read." The Arabic verb *qara'a*, the imperative of which is used here, means both to read and to recite. The angel took hold of the Prophet and pressed him so vehemently that he was nearly suffocated and repeated his command, "Recite!" The Prophet again answered, "I cannot read." A second time the angel pressed him vehemently and repeated the command for the third time. The Prophet then answered, "What shall I recite?" The angel said "Recite in the name of your Lord," and so on, until he recited these verses. Shaking with fear, the Prophet returned to his wife Khadījah exclaiming, "cover me up, cover me up!" After his fear had subsided, he related his experience to his wife, who reassured him with the words, "No, by God, be of good cheer, for God would never disgrace you. You surely treat your next-of-kin with kindness. You always speak the truth and endure weariness patiently. You receive the guest hospitably and lend assistance in times of adversity."

Khadījah then took him to a cousin of hers, Waraqah b. Nawfal, who had accepted Christianity and read the Scriptures in Hebrew, and could read and write Arabic as well. When Muḥammad told the old man what had happened to him, Waraqah exclaimed, "This is the sacred law *(nāmūs)* which God sent down to Moses! Would that I were still young! Would that I were alive when your people shall drive you out!: The Prophet asked, "Will they drive me out?" "Yes," Waraqah answered. "No one ever came with that which you now bring but that his people did him harm. Were I to live to see your day, I would support you with all my strength." Soon after, Waraqah died.

(٩٦) سُورَةُ العَلَقِ مَكِّيَّة
وآياتها ١٩ وهي أوّل ما نزل من القرآن

بِسْمِ اللهِ الرَّحْمَنِ الرَّحِيمِ

اقْرَأْ بِاسْمِ رَبِّكَ الَّذِى خَلَقَ ﴿١﴾ خَلَقَ الْإِنْسَـنَ
مِنْ عَلَقٍ ﴿٢﴾ اقْرَأْ وَرَبُّكَ الْأَكْرَمُ ﴿٣﴾ الَّذِى عَلَّمَ
بِالْقَلَمِ ﴿٤﴾ عَلَّمَ الْإِنْسَـنَ مَا لَمْ يَعْلَمْ ﴿٥﴾ كَلَّا إِنَّ

6. No, indeed, but man waxes arrogant,

7. for he thinks himself to be self-sufficient.

8. Surely to your Lord shall be the return.

9. Have you considered him who forbids

10. a servant when he prays?

11. Have you considered whether he is guided aright,

12. or that he enjoins fear of God?

13. Have you considered whether he cries lies and turns away?

14. Does he not know that God sees?

15. No, indeed, if he does not desist, we shall seize him by the forelock,

16. a lying and sinful forelock.

17. So let him call upon his concourse!

18. We shall call the guardians [of Hell]!

19. No, indeed, do not obey him; rather prostrate yourself and draw near.*

(v. 9-19) These verses were revealed concerning Abū Jahl who was one of the bitterest enemies of the Prophet. He sought to prevent the Prophet from praying in the Kaaba, threatening him with bodily harm. At the close of the recitation of this *sūrah*, the reciter and anyone present must prostrate themselves.

كَلَّا إِنَّ ٱلْإِنسَـٰنَ لَيَطْغَىٰٓ ۝ أَن رَّءَاهُ ٱسْتَغْنَىٰٓ ۝ إِنَّ إِلَىٰ رَبِّكَ ٱلرُّجْعَىٰٓ ۝ أَرَءَيْتَ ٱلَّذِى يَنْهَىٰ ۝ عَبْدًا إِذَا صَلَّىٰٓ ۝ أَرَءَيْتَ إِن كَانَ عَلَى ٱلْهُدَىٰٓ ۝ أَوْ أَمَرَ بِٱلتَّقْوَىٰٓ ۝ أَرَءَيْتَ إِن كَذَّبَ وَتَوَلَّىٰٓ ۝ أَلَمْ يَعْلَم بِأَنَّ ٱللَّهَ يَرَىٰ ۝ كَلَّا لَئِن لَّمْ يَنتَهِ لَنَسْفَعًۢا بِٱلنَّاصِيَةِ ۝ نَاصِيَةٍ كَاذِبَةٍ خَاطِئَةٍ ۝ فَلْيَدْعُ نَادِيَهُۥ ۝ سَنَدْعُ ٱلزَّبَانِيَةَ ۝ كَلَّا لَا تُطِعْهُ وَٱسْجُدْ وَٱقْتَرِب ۩ ۝

Sūrah 97
al-Qadr
(Determination)

This *sūrah*, which consists of five verses, was revealed in Mecca after *sūrah* 80, 'Abasa. Its main themes are:

1. A declaration of the blessed Night of Determination, the night the Qur'ān was sent down; and

2. The descent of the angels on this night to execute the commands of their Lord.

The Qur'ān clearly refers to the time of the revelation of the Qur'ān in three verses: two in Mecca and one in Medina. The earliest reference is the one in this *sūrah*, as will be seen below. The second is in *sūrah* 44: 3 which reads, "We have surely sent it [the Qur'ān] down on a blessed night." The third is in *sūrah* 2: 185 which declares, "The month of Ramaḍān is the month in which the Qur'ān was sent down ..." In yet a fourth verse we have an allusion to this point in the words, "If you have truly accepted faith in God and what we sent down to our servants on the day of the Criterion (*furqān*), the day on which the two parties met (i.e., the battle of Badr) ..." (*sūrah* 8: 43). On the basis of this verse it may be concluded that this verse indicates that God sent down the Qur'ān to his apostle on the same day when the two parties met in the battle of Badr. It is clear from all this that this night was Friday night, the seventeenth of Ramaḍān. According to most sound *ḥadīth* traditions the actual Night of Determination falls every year on one of the last ten nights of Ramaḍān, most probably on one of the odd nights. It is celebrated by most Muslims on the eve of the 27th of Ramaḍān.

117

In the name of God the All Merciful, the Compassionate

1. We have surely sent it down on the Night of Determination.

2. Would that you knew what the Night of Determination is!

3. The Night of Determination is greater than a thousand months.*

4. In it the angels and the Spirit descend by leave of their Lord with every command.*

5. Peace it is until the rising of the dawn.

(v. 3) i.e., prayers, fasting and other devotional acts performed on it are better than those of a thousand months. It is related that the Prophet said at the beginning of Ramadān, "The month of Ramadān is upon you. It is the blessed month whose fast God has made obligatory on you. In it the gates of Paradise are opened and the gates of the Fire are closed, and Satans are bound in chains. It is a night better than a thousand months. Anyone deprived of its blessing has been truly deprived".

(v. 4) According to some commentators, the Spirit here refers to Gabriel. According to others, it refers to an unspecified great angel.

(٩٧) سُورَةُ الْقَدْرِ مَكِّيَّة
وَآيَاتُهَا ٥ نَزَلَتْ بَعْدَ عَبَسَ

بِسْمِ اللهِ الرَّحْمٰنِ الرَّحِيمِ

إِنَّا أَنْزَلْنَاهُ فِي لَيْلَةِ الْقَدْرِ ﴿١﴾ وَمَا أَدْرَاكَ مَا لَيْلَةُ
الْقَدْرِ ﴿٢﴾ لَيْلَةُ الْقَدْرِ خَيْرٌ مِنْ أَلْفِ شَهْرٍ ﴿٣﴾ تَنَزَّلُ
الْمَلَائِكَةُ وَالرُّوحُ فِيهَا بِإِذْنِ رَبِّهِمْ مِنْ كُلِّ أَمْرٍ ﴿٤﴾
سَلَامٌ هِيَ حَتَّى مَطْلَعِ الْفَجْرِ ﴿٥﴾

Sūrah 98
al-Bayyinah
(The Clear Sign)

This *sūrah* consists of eight verses and was revealed either in Medina, according to most commentators, or in Mecca, as may be suggested by its theme and subject matter. The date of its revelation is uncertain. The *sūrah* deals with two main subjects.

1. The first is the assertion that the rejectors of faith among the people of the Book and the Associators (the Meccan Arabs) will not desist from opposing the new faith of Islām until they see a clear sign of revelation and apostleship, although they were enjoined by God to worship Him alone and follow the straight way of faith (verses 1-5).

2. The second theme is the usual Qur'ānic contrast between the rejectors of faith and their final punishment and the people of faith and their reward in Paradise and the pleasure of God with them (verses 6-8).

In the name of God, the All-Merciful, the Compassionate

1. The rejectors of faith of the people of the Book and the Associators will not desist until a clear sign comes to them,

2. a messenger from God reciting pages purified,

3. in which are contained true writings.*

4. Those who were given the Book did not fall into schism except after a clear sign had come to them.

(v. 2-3) The apostle here intended is Muḥammad and the purified pages are the Qur'ān.

120

(٩٨) سُورَةُ الْبَيِّنَة مَدَنِيَّة
وَآيَاتُهَا ٨ نَزَلَتْ بَعْدَ الطَّلَاق

بِسْمِ اللهِ الرَّحْمَنِ الرَّحِيمِ

لَمْ يَكُنِ ٱلَّذِينَ كَفَرُواْ مِنْ أَهْلِ ٱلْكِتَـٰبِ وَٱلْمُشْرِكِينَ مُنفَكِّينَ حَتَّىٰ تَأْتِيَهُمُ ٱلْبَيِّنَةُ ﴿١﴾ رَسُولٌ مِّنَ ٱللهِ يَتْلُواْ صُحُفًا مُّطَهَّرَةً ﴿٢﴾ فِيهَا كُتُبٌ قَيِّمَةٌ ﴿٣﴾ وَمَا تَفَرَّقَ ٱلَّذِينَ أُوتُواْ ٱلْكِتَـٰبَ إِلَّا مِنۢ بَعْدِ مَا جَآءَتْهُمُ ٱلْبَيِّنَةُ ﴿٤﴾ وَمَآ أُمِرُوٓاْ إِلَّا لِيَعْبُدُواْ ٱللهَ مُخْلِصِينَ لَهُ

5. Yet they were commanded only to worship God, sincere in their faith towards Him; to be of pure religion, establishing regular worship and giving the obligatory alms [zakāt], for that indeed is the upright religion.*

6. Surely those of the people of the Book and the Associators who have rejected faith shall be in the Fire of Hell forever. These are the worst of creation,

7. except those who have faith and perform good deeds—these are the best of creation.

8. Their reward with their Lord shall be gardens of Eden in which rivers flow, therein to dwell forever. God is well pleased with them and they are well pleased with Him. That shall be for him who fears his Lord.

(v. 5) The word *ḥunafā'*, the singular of which is *ḥanīf*, means "one who inclines to one side because of a foot deformity." It is used in the Qur'ān and later Muslim tradition to mean one who inclines himself away from idolatry to the pure faith in one God. Thus Abraham is described in the Qur'ān as a *ḥanīf*, a man of pure faith (see Q. 2: 135; and 6: 79 and 161). The words *dīn al-qayyimah* (upright religion) refer to Abraham and his descendants, the community following the upright religion. It is also the religion taught by the scriptures mentioned in v. 2.

ٱلدِّينَ حُنَفَآءَ وَيُقِيمُواْ ٱلصَّلَوٰةَ وَيُؤْتُواْ ٱلزَّكَوٰةَ وَذَٰلِكَ دِينُ ٱلْقَيِّمَةِ ۝ إِنَّ ٱلَّذِينَ كَفَرُواْ مِنْ أَهْلِ ٱلْكِتَٰبِ وَٱلْمُشْرِكِينَ فِى نَارِ جَهَنَّمَ خَٰلِدِينَ فِيهَآ أُوْلَٰٓئِكَ هُمْ شَرُّ ٱلْبَرِيَّةِ ۝ إِنَّ ٱلَّذِينَ ءَامَنُواْ وَعَمِلُواْ ٱلصَّٰلِحَٰتِ أُوْلَٰٓئِكَ هُمْ خَيْرُ ٱلْبَرِيَّةِ ۝ جَزَآؤُهُمْ عِندَ رَبِّهِمْ جَنَّٰتُ عَدْنٍ تَجْرِى مِن تَحْتِهَا ٱلْأَنْهَٰرُ خَٰلِدِينَ فِيهَآ أَبَدًا رَّضِىَ ٱللَّهُ عَنْهُمْ وَرَضُواْ عَنْهُ ذَٰلِكَ لِمَنْ خَشِىَ رَبَّهُۥ ۝

123

Sūrah 99
al-Zalzalah
(The Earthquake)

This *sūrah* consists of eight verses and was revealed in Medina not long after the Prophet migrated. It is a sustained and powerful depiction of the fearful events of the Day of Judgment when all men shall be gathered together to reap the fruits of their deeds. It is related that this *surāh* equals half of the Qur'ān in its meaning and comprehensiveness.

In the name of God the All Merciful, the Compassionate

1. When the earth shall be shaken with a great quake,

2. and the earth yields up its burdens,

3. and man exclaims, "What has happened to it!"

4. On that day it shall recount its tidings--

5. as your Lord had inspired it.

6. On that day humankind shall return in scatterings to be shown their deeds.

7. Whoever does an atom's weight of good shall then see it,

8. and whoever does an atom's weight of evil shall then see it.

(٩٩) سُورَةُ الزَّلْزَلَةِ مَكِّيَّة
وآيَاتُهَا ٨ نَزَلَتْ بَعْدَ النِّسَاء

بِسْمِ اللَّهِ الرَّحْمَنِ الرَّحِيمِ

إِذَا زُلْزِلَتِ الْأَرْضُ زِلْزَالَهَا ﴿١﴾ وَأَخْرَجَتِ الْأَرْضُ

أَثْقَالَهَا ﴿٢﴾ وَقَالَ الْإِنْسَانُ مَا لَهَا ﴿٣﴾ يَوْمَئِذٍ

تُحَدِّثُ أَخْبَارَهَا ﴿٤﴾ بِأَنَّ رَبَّكَ أَوْحَى لَهَا ﴿٥﴾ يَوْمَئِذٍ

يَصْدُرُ النَّاسُ أَشْتَاتًا لِيُرَوْا أَعْمَالَهُمْ ﴿٦﴾ فَمَن يَعْمَلْ

مِثْقَالَ ذَرَّةٍ خَيْرًا يَرَهُ ﴿٧﴾ وَمَن يَعْمَلْ مِثْقَالَ ذَرَّةٍ

شَرًّا يَرَهُ ﴿٨﴾

Sūrah 100
al-'Ādiyāt
(The Chargers)

This *sūrah* was revealed in Mecca after *sūrah* 103, *al-'Aṣr*. It consists of eleven verses and may be divided into three sections.

1. The first is a series of oaths by horses in the state of war, engaged in intense activity (verses 1-5).

2. This is followed by the assertion that man is ungrateful to God and loves wealth with a passion (verses 6-8).

3. The third section is a reminder to such people of the Day of Resurrection when all thoughts shall be disclosed and God will encompass all things in knowledge and power (verses 9-11).

In the name of God, the All-Merciful, the Compassionate

1. By the chargers, snorting!

2. By the strikers [with their hooves] sparking!

3. By the raiders at dawn,

4. raising therewith a veil of dust:

5. Forcing therewith their way into the midst of the host!*

(v. 1-5) Early authorities have differed as to what is intended by these oaths. It is related on the authority of 'Alī that the reference here is to the battle of Badr where camels rather than horses were employed. In yet another tradition also attributed to 'Alī, these oaths are said to depict the pilgrims as they rush on their animals from Mt. 'Arafāt to Muzdalifah (one of the pilgrimage stations below) and from there to Mīna (another pilgrimage station). The view most widely accepted, however, is that horses are here intended, as the text clearly indicates.

(۱۰۰) سُورَةُ الْعَادِيَاتِ مَكِّيَّة
وَآيَاتُهَا ۱۱ نَزَلَتْ بَعْدَ الْعَصْرِ

بِسْمِ اللهِ الرَّحْمَنِ الرَّحِيمِ

وَالْعَادِيَاتِ ضَبْحًا ۝ فَالْمُورِيَاتِ قَدْحًا ۝

فَالْمُغِيرَاتِ صُبْحًا ۝ فَأَثَرْنَ بِهِ نَقْعًا ۝ فَوَسَطْنَ

بِهِ جَمْعًا ۝ إِنَّ الْإِنْسَانَ لِرَبِّهِ لَكَنُودٌ ۝ وَإِنَّهُ

In the name of God the All Merciful, the Compassionate

6. Surely man is ungrateful to his Lord,

7. and to this he is indeed a witness.

8. He surely loves wealth with a great passion.

9. Does he not know that when that which is in the tombs shall be overturned,

10. and that which is in the breasts shall be brought out:

11. that on that day their Lord shall be fully aware of them!

عَلَىٰ ذَٰلِكَ لَشَهِيدٌ ۞ وَإِنَّهُ لِحُبِّ ٱلْخَيْرِ لَشَدِيدٌ ۞

۞ أَفَلَا يَعْلَمُ إِذَا بُعْثِرَ مَا فِى ٱلْقُبُورِ ۞ وَحُصِّلَ

مَا فِى ٱلصُّدُورِ ۞ إِنَّ رَبَّهُم بِهِمْ يَوْمَئِذٍ لَّخَبِيرٌ ۞

Sūrah 101
al-Qāri‘ah
(The Pounder)

This *sūrah* was revealed in Mecca after *sūrah* 106, Quraysh. It consists of eleven brief verses painting a vivid and fearful picture of the Day of Resurrection, which is here called "the pounder" or "crushing catastrophe." Mountains shall be crushed like fluffed tufts of wool, and men scattered like troubled moths. The *sūrah* concludes with a brief description of the lot of the people of faith and that of the rejectors of faith, each according to the scales of their good or evil deeds.

In the name of God, the All-Merciful, the Compassionate

1. O the pounder!

2. What is the pounder!

3. Would that you knew what the pounder is!

4. It is a day on which men shall be like scattered moths,

5. and the mountains shall be like fluffed tufts of wool.

6. As for him whose scales shall weigh heavy [with good deeds],

7. he shall be in a pleasing life.

8. But as for him whose scales shall weigh light,

9. his mother shall be the pit.*

10. Would that you knew what it is,

11. a fire hotly blazing!

(v. 9) The word "mother" is used here to denote the place or abode or that which would totally envelope a person.

(١٠١) سُورَةُ ٱلْقَارِعَةِ مَكِّيَّة
وَآيَاتُهَا ١١ نَزَلَتْ بَعْدَ قُرَيْشٍ

بِسْمِ ٱللَّهِ ٱلرَّحْمَٰنِ ٱلرَّحِيمِ

ٱلْقَارِعَةُ ﴿١﴾ مَا ٱلْقَارِعَةُ ﴿٢﴾ وَمَآ أَدْرَىٰكَ مَا ٱلْقَارِعَةُ ﴿٣﴾

يَوْمَ يَكُونُ ٱلنَّاسُ كَٱلْفَرَاشِ ٱلْمَبْثُوثِ ﴿٤﴾ وَتَكُونُ

ٱلْجِبَالُ كَٱلْعِهْنِ ٱلْمَنفُوشِ ﴿٥﴾ فَأَمَّا مَن ثَقُلَتْ

مَوَٰزِينُهُۥ ﴿٦﴾ فَهُوَ فِي عِيشَةٍ رَّاضِيَةٍ ﴿٧﴾ وَأَمَّا مَنْ خَفَّتْ

مَوَٰزِينُهُۥ ﴿٨﴾ فَأُمُّهُۥ هَاوِيَةٌ ﴿٩﴾ وَمَآ أَدْرَىٰكَ مَاهِيَهْ ﴿١٠﴾

نَارٌ حَامِيَةٌۢ ﴿١١﴾

Sūrah 102
al-Takāthur
(Multiplying)

This *sūrah* was revealed in Mecca after *sūrah* 108, *al-Kawthar*. It consists of eight verses and is a warning to those who are occupied in this life with the multiplying of wealth and offspring. It is related that the Prophet said, "Three things follow a dead man to his grave; two of them return and one remains with him. He is followed by his family, his wealth and deeds. His family and wealth return and his deeds stay with him."

In the name of God, the All-Merciful, the Compassionate

1. Multiplying [of wealth and offspring] had diverted you,

2. until you visited the tombs.

3. No, indeed, you shall know!

4. Again, no indeed, you shall know!

5. No, indeed, if you only knew the knowledge of certainty;

6. you will see the blazing Fire.

7. For you shall surely see it with the eye of certainty.

8. Then will you be questioned concerning true bliss.*

(v. 8) The word *na'īm* (bliss) here refers to God's favors towards humankind in this life, such as health, sound faculties, shelter and food and all the essential comforts of life.

---

(١٠٢) سُورَةُ التَّكَاثُرِ مَكِّيَّةٌ
وَآيَاتُهَا ٨ نَزَلَتْ بَعْدَ الْكَوْثَرِ

بِسْمِ اللهِ الرَّحْمَنِ الرَّحِيمِ

أَلْهَكُمُ التَّكَاثُرُ ۞ حَتَّى زُرْتُمُ الْمَقَابِرَ ۞ كَلَّا سَوْفَ

تَعْلَمُونَ ۞ ثُمَّ كَلَّا سَوْفَ تَعْلَمُونَ ۞ كَلَّا لَوْ تَعْلَمُونَ

عِلْمَ الْيَقِينِ ۞ لَتَرَوُنَّ الْجَحِيمَ ۞ ثُمَّ لَتَرَوُنَّهَا عَيْنَ

الْيَقِينِ ۞ ثُمَّ لَتُسْأَلُنَّ يَوْمَئِذٍ عَنِ النَّعِيمِ ۞

Sūrah 103
al-'Aṣr
(Passing Time or Afternoon)

This *sūrah* was revealed in Mecca after *sūrah* 94: *al-Inshirāḥ,* and takes its title from the first word of the first verse. Commentators have differed as to whether the word *'aṣr* here means afternoon, or time in the sense of successive ages. The latter seems to be the most likely interpretation.

It has been said that had people pondered this *sūrah,* it would have sufficed them. This *sūrah* of three brief verses presents a complete philosophy of life and history. It is related that every time two of the Companions of the Prophet met, they did not part until one of them had recited the *sūrah* and greeted his fellow the salutation of peace.

In the name of God the All Merciful, the Compassionate

1. By [passing] time!

2. Surely man is in a state of loss,

3. except those who have faith and perform righteous deeds, and who enjoin upon one another [abiding by the] truth, and enjoin upon one another steadfastness.

(١٠٣) سُورَة العَصرِ مكيّة
وآياتها ٣ نزلت بعد الشرح

بِسمِ اللهِ الرَّحمٰنِ الرَّحِيمِ

وَالعَصرِ ۝ إِنَّ الإِنسَٰنَ لَفِى خُسرٍ ۝ إِلَّا الَّذِينَ ءَامَنُوا۟ وَعَمِلُوا۟ الصَّٰلِحَٰتِ وَتَوَاصَوا۟ بِالحَقِّ وَتَوَاصَوا۟ بِالصَّبرِ ۝

Sūrah 104
al-Humazah
(The Slanderer)

This *sūrah* was revealed early in Mecca after *sūrah* 75, *al-Qiyāmah* (Resurrection). It is related that it was revealed concerning a man called al-Akhnas b. Shurayq, who used to slander people both to their faces and behind their backs. It is also related that the *sūrah* was revealed concerning al-Walīd b. al-Mughīrah, a man well-known for his hostility to the Prophet in the early years of his mission. Al-Walīd used to slander the Prophet directly and in his absence.

This *sūrah,* consisting of nine verses, presents a vivid picture of a person who is of such small soul that his wealth blinds him to the truth and even to the common decency in human relations. Even though the *sūrah* may depict a particular human being during the formative years of Muslim history, it applies to such people at all times and places. Such men are destined to a crushing torment, from which they shall have no escape.

In the name of God the All Merciful, the Compassionate

1. Woe to every slanderer, backbiter—

2. who gathers wealth, greedily counting it over and over.

3. Does he think that his wealth will make him immortal?

4. No, indeed, but he shall be thrown into the crusher.

5. Would that you knew what the crusher is!

6. It is the Fire of God, set ablaze,

7. which penetrates into innermost hearts.

8. It will close in upon them,

9. in columns outstretched.

(١٠٤) سُورَةُ الهُمَزَةِ مَكِّيَّةٌ
وَآياتُها ٩ نَزَلَتْ بَعْدَ القِيَامَةِ

بِسْمِ اللهِ الرَّحْمَنِ الرَّحِيمِ

وَيْلٌ لِّكُلِّ هُمَزَةٍ لُّمَزَةٍ ۝ ٱلَّذِى جَمَعَ مَالًا وَعَدَّدَهُ ۝

يَحْسَبُ أَنَّ مَالَهُۥ أَخْلَدَهُۥ ۝ كَلَّا لَيُنبَذَنَّ فِى ٱلْحُطَمَةِ ۝

وَمَآ أَدْرَىٰكَ مَا ٱلْحُطَمَةُ ۝ نَارُ ٱللهِ ٱلْمُوقَدَةُ ۝

ٱلَّتِى تَطَّلِعُ عَلَى ٱلْأَفْـِٔدَةِ ۝ إِنَّهَا عَلَيْهِم مُّؤْصَدَةٌ ۝

فِى عَمَدٍ مُّمَدَّدَةٍ ۝

٣

Sūrah 105
al-Fīl
(The Elephant)

This *sūrah* was revealed in Mecca after *sūrah* 109, *al-Kāfirūn*. It takes its title from the reference to the army of the elephant, which is the main subject of this brief *sūrah*.

The *sūrah* consists of five verses depicting the plight of the army of the elephant, which was utterly destroyed by God. It is related that Abraha, the Abyssinian general who ruled Yemen, built a great church in Ṣanʿāʾ, wishing by this to divert pilgrimage from the Kaaba. As the Arabs of the Ḥijāz refused to give up their allegiance to the ancient shrine, Abraha gathered a large army which he headed on a great elephant. The appearance of a war elephant was a new phenomenon to the Arabs, hence its specific mention.

Abraha is said to have advanced against the Kaaba in the year 70 A.D., the year in which, according to tradition, the Prophet Muḥammad was born. As the army encamped outside the sacred area around the Kaaba, the men were afflicted by a plague, which the *sūrah* graphically describes. The *sūrah* presents the destruction of Abraha's army as a Divine miracle. Later commentators, on the basis of references to an epidemic of smallpox which appeared in Arabia for the first time in that year, concluded that it was simply the germs of that epidemic which the birds referred to in this *sūrah* carried on tiny pebbles and with which they pelted the invading army. The purpose of the *sūrah* is to show God's favor towards the tribe of Quraysh of Mecca and His protection of the Sacred House, which was to regain its original sanctity with the coming of Islām. Thus whether the miracle was, as tradition asserts, that the tiny pebbles penetrated the person pelted with them through his head and out through his mount, or that they carried the germs of a deadly disease, the miracle of direct Divine intervention remains valid. This is the real aim of the *sūrah* and the tradition interpreting it.

In the name of God the All Merciful, the Compassionate

1. Have you not considered how your Lord dealt with the people of the elephant?

2. Did He not turn their evil scheming to no avail?

3. For He sent against them birds in great flocks,

4. which hurled at them stones of baked clay.

5. He thus made them as dry leaves chewed up.

(١٠٥) سُورَةِ الفِيلَ مَكِّيَّة
وآياتها ٥ نزلت بَعْدَ الكَافِرُون

بِسْمِ اللهِ الرَّحْمٰنِ الرَّحِيمِ

أَلَمْ تَرَ كَيْفَ فَعَلَ رَبُّكَ بِأَصْحَابِ الْفِيلِ ۝ أَلَمْ يَجْعَلْ كَيْدَهُمْ فِى تَضْلِيلٍ ۝ وَأَرْسَلَ عَلَيْهِمْ طَيْرًا أَبَابِيلَ ۝ تَرْمِيهِمْ بِحِجَارَةٍ مِّن سِجِّيلٍ ۝ فَجَعَلَهُمْ كَعَصْفٍ مَّأْكُولٍ ۝

Sūrah 106
Quraysh

This *sūrah* was revealed in Mecca. According to some early authorities and notably the well-known Companion and commentator Ubayy B. Ka'b, this and the previous *sūrah* are one continuous text. In his *mushaf*, Ubayy did not separate the two *sūrahs* with the invocation, "In the name of God ...." Yet even though they follow one another in the official rescension of the Qur'ān, according to many commentators they are separated chronologically by nine *sūrahs*. The two *sūrahs*, however, are so close in meaning and purpose that the beginning of the second seems to follow from the previous one and explain its purpose.

The *sūrah* consists of four brief verses which allude to the path of safety between Quraysh and their neighbors, enabling them to undertake the two annual caravans. Thus in winter they journeyed east to Yemen where they bought spices and other commodities coming from India and beyond. These they carried in the summer west to Syria where they sold them and brought back agricultural products. The *sūrah* first implies that God saved the Quraysh from the superior might of Abraha and preserved the Kaaba which was a source of prestige and economic well-being for them. Hence, the *sūrah* concludes, they must worship the Lord of the Sacred House alone in gratitude for all His favors towards them.

In the name of God the All Merciful, the Compassionate

1. This, for the sake of the pact of safety of Quraysh,*

2. for the sake of their safety during the winter and summer journeys.

3. Let them then worship the Lord of this house,

4. who provided them with food against hunger, and made them secure from fear.

(v. 1) The word "this" denoting the article *li* means We [God] prevented the elephant from harming Mecca and destroyed the people of the elephant in order that the security of the Quraysh in their town might be assured.

(١٠٦) سُورَةُ قُرَيْشٍ مَكِّيَّة
وَآيَاتُهَا ٤ نَزَلَتْ بَعْدَ التِّينِ

بِسْمِ اللَّهِ الرَّحْمَنِ الرَّحِيمِ

لِإِيلَافِ قُرَيْشٍ ﴿١﴾ إِۦلَٰفِهِمْ رِحْلَةَ الشِّتَآءِ وَالصَّيْفِ ﴿٢﴾ فَلْيَعْبُدُوا رَبَّ هَٰذَا الْبَيْتِ ﴿٣﴾ الَّذِىٓ أَطْعَمَهُم مِّن جُوعٍ وَءَامَنَهُم مِّنْ خَوْفٍۭ ﴿٤﴾

Sūrah 107
al-Māʿūn
(Assistance)

This *sūrah* was, according to some authorities, revealed early in Mecca after *sūrah* 102, *al-Takāthur*. According to others, the first three of its seven verses were revealed in Mecca and the remaining four in Medina. It is probable that the entire *sūrah* was revealed in Medina, because the subject it treats, namely heedlessness and hypocrisy in the performance of prayers, was unknown to the small group of Muslims of Mecca.

The word *māʿūn* from which the *sūrah* takes its title is the last word of the *sūrah*. It means literally "vessel" or "utensil" such as a pot or axe. In its widest sense the word *māʿūn* means any act of kindness, charity or assistance which a person may do to another by sharing with him the use of such items of daily need.

In the name of God the All Merciful, the Compassionate

1. Have you considered him who gives the lie to the [Day of] Recompense!

2. Such is he who repulses the orphan,

3. and who does not urge the feeding of the needy.

4. Woe to them who pray

5. but who are negligent in their prayers;*

6. those who make a show,

7. and withhold assistance.

(v. 4-5) Two closely related interpretations of these two verses have been offered by commentators. The first is that such people are negligent in offering their prayers at the right time. The second is that even though they offer their prayers in the proper time, they are nonetheless negligent in their proper devotions. They only perform mechanical movements to make a show before others while they themselves are not touched by their prayers.

(١٠٧) سُورَة الماعون
مكية ثلاث الآيات الأول مدنية البقية
وآيالها ٧ نزلت بعد التكاثر

بِسْمِ اللَّهِ الرَّحْمَنِ الرَّحِيمِ

أَرَأَيْتَ ٱلَّذِى يُكَذِّبُ بِٱلدِّينِ ﴿١﴾ فَذَلِكَ ٱلَّذِى يَدُعُّ ٱلْيَتِيمَ ﴿٢﴾ وَلَا يَحُضُّ عَلَى طَعَامِ ٱلْمِسْكِينِ ﴿٣﴾ فَوَيْلٌ لِّلْمُصَلِّينَ ﴿٤﴾ ٱلَّذِينَ هُمْ عَن صَلَاتِهِمْ سَاهُونَ ﴿٥﴾ ٱلَّذِينَ هُمْ يُرَاؤُونَ ﴿٦﴾ وَيَمْنَعُونَ ٱلْمَاعُونَ ﴿٧﴾

145

Sūrah 108
al-Kawthar
(Abundance)

This is the shortest *sūrah* of the Qur'ān, consisting of three brief verses. It was revealed in Mecca after *sūrah* 100, *al-'Ādiyat,* or perhaps in Medina at an uncertain date. The word *kawthar* (abundance) from which the *sūrah* takes its title has been identified as a river or large basin of Paradisial waters which will be given to the Prophet Muḥammad on the Day of Ressurection.

According to tradition, the revelation (*waḥī*) of the Qur'ān always came to the Prophet in the waking state. In a well-known tradition reported on the authority of 'Ā'ishah, there is the suggestion that dream visions preceded proper revelations (see the Introduction). This *sūrah*, however, is said to have come to the Prophet in a dream. It is related on the authority of Anas b. Mālik (a well-known Companion) that one day the Prophet fell asleep among his companions. He woke up smiling. When asked what made him smile, he replied, "Just now a *sūrah* was sent down to me." He then recited the *sūrah*. Commentators are unanimous in asserting that the reason for the revelation of this *sūrah* was the Meccans' taunting of the Prophet for not having male children, calling him *al-abtar,* meaning "one who is cut off, having no male heir to carry on his name".

In the name of God the All Merciful, the Compassionate

1. We have surely given you abundance!

2. Pray, therefore, to your Lord and offer your sacrifice.*

3. Surely he who hates you, he shall be cut off.

(v. 2) According to some commentators, the sacrifice here mentioned means not the slaughter of an animal but the offering of prayers while pointing one's neck (which is the place of slaughter) to the Qiblah, or direction of prayer; or placing the hands below the neck. The most widely accepted view, however, is that of offering animal sacrifice along with the prayer and completing one's total devotions to God.

146

(١٠٨) سُورَةُ الكَوْثَرِ مَكِّيَّة
وَآياتُها ٣ نزلَتْ بعدَ العَادِياتِ

بِسْمِ اللهِ الرَّحْمَنِ الرَّحِيمِ

إِنَّا أَعْطَيْنَاكَ الْكَوْثَرَ ۝ فَصَلِّ لِرَبِّكَ وَانْحَرْ ۝

إِنَّ شَانِئَكَ هُوَ الْأَبْتَرُ ۝

147

Sūrah 109
al-Kāfirūn
(The Rejectors of Faith)

This *sūrah* consists of six verses expressing one single theme, namely that no one or thing may be worshipped beside God. It was revealed in Mecca after *sūrah* 107, *al-Māʿūn*. We are told that the Meccans of Quraysh suggested to the Prophet that he worship their gods for one year and they worship God for the next. In this way, both he and they would benefit from the worship of each other's religion. This *sūrah* was therefore revealed to emphasize the rejection of the Prophet and the Muslims after him of every kind of association *(shirk)* of any one or thing with God.

It is reported that the Prophet used to recite this and *sūrah* 112 in his dawn prayers. It is also related that he recited them in the prayers of the pilgrimage rite. A man is said to have asked the Prophet to teach him something to recite before retiring to sleep. The Prophet said, "When you retire to your bed, you shall say 'O you rejectors of faith ....' to its end for it is an immunity from association [of other things with God]"

In the name of God the All Merciful, the Compassionate

1. Say: O you rejectors of faith,

2. I do not worship what you worship.

3. Nor are you worshipping what I worship.

4. Nor will I worship what you are worshipping.

5. Nor will you worship what I am worshipping.

6. To you belongs your faith and to me belongs my faith.

(١٠٩) سُورَةِ الْكَافِرُونَ مَكِّيَّة
وَآيَاتُهَا ٦ نَزَلَتْ بَعْدَ الْمَاعُونَ

بِسْمِ اللهِ الرَّحْمَنِ الرَّحِيمِ

قُلْ يَا أَيُّهَا الْكَافِرُونَ ﴿١﴾ لَا أَعْبُدُ مَا تَعْبُدُونَ ﴿٢﴾

وَلَا أَنتُمْ عَابِدُونَ مَا أَعْبُدُ ﴿٣﴾ وَلَا أَنَا عَابِدٌ مَّا عَبَدتُّمْ ﴿٤﴾

وَلَا أَنتُمْ عَابِدُونَ مَا أَعْبُدُ ﴿٥﴾ لَكُمْ دِينُكُمْ وَلِيَ دِينِ ﴿٦﴾

149

Surah 110
al-Nasr
(Support)

This *sūrah,* which consists of three verses, was the last complete *sūrah* to be revealed of the Qur'ān. It was revealed during the farewell pilgrimage in Mīna (a station of the pilgrimage outside Mecca) in the tenth year of the Hijrah (632), about two months before the Prophet's death. Before the present *sūrah,* the words, "Today I have perfected your religion for you and have completed my favor toward you and have accepted Islām as a religion for you" (*Surah 5:3*) were revealed. Thus the present *sūrah* indicates that the work of the Prophet had been accomplished.

It is reported that 'Umar b. al-Khaṭṭāb, the second caliph, once asked Ibn 'Abbās about the meaning of this *sūrah.* The latter answered, "It was a sign of the approaching end of the life of the Apostle of God. God said, 'When support from God comes and victory, that shall be the sign of your end. Proclaim therefore the praise of your Lord and seek His forgiveness for He is truly relenting.'". On the basis of this *sūrah* the Prophet and later Muslim rulers offered on entering a newly conquered city the prayer of conquest (*salāt al-fath*). This prayer consists of eight *rak'ahs* (units, performed in groups of two *rak'ahs.*)

In the name of God the All Merciful, the Compassionate

1. When support from God comes, and victory,

2. and you see men enter into the religion of God in throngs,

3. proclaim the praise of your Lord and seek His forgiveness, for He is truly relenting.*

(v. 1-3) The reference here is to the conquest of Mecca. Classical tradition reports that the neighboring tribes were reluctant to enter into Islām because they felt that so long as the Prophet's own city remained outside his domain, his authority remained in doubt. Thus when Mecca was conquered, "they entered into the religion of God in throngs," so that within two years every inhabitant of Arabia declared Islām.

(١١٠) سُورَة النَّصر نزلت بمنى في حجة الوداع
فتعد مدنية وهي آخر ما نزل من السور
وآياتها ٣ نزلت بعد التوبة

بِسْمِ اللهِ الرَّحْمٰنِ الرَّحِيمِ

إِذَا جَآءَ نَصْرُ اللهِ وَالْفَتْحُ ﴿١﴾ وَرَأَيْتَ النَّاسَ يَدْخُلُونَ

فِي دِينِ اللهِ أَفْوَاجًا ﴿٢﴾ فَسَبِّحْ بِحَمْدِ رَبِّكَ وَاسْتَغْفِرْهُ

إِنَّهُ كَانَ تَوَّابًا ﴿٣﴾

Sūrah 111
al-Lahab
(The Flame)

This *sūrah* was revealed in Mecca after *sūrah* 48, *al-Fatḥ* (conquest), and consists of five verses. The *sūrah* is a condemnation of an uncle of the Prophet called 'Abd al-'Uzza (servant of al-'Uzza, one of the three godesses of Mecca worshipped before Islām). Because of his bright countenance he was nicknamed Abū Lahab (the man of flame). It is related concerning the occasion of the revelation of this *sūrah* that one day the Prophet climbed one of the hills around Mecca and raised the cry of fear usually raised at the approach of an enemy. When the Meccans gathered below he said, "If I were to tell you that an enemy shall come upon you in the morning or evening, would you believe me?" They answered, "Yes." He continued, "I am come to warn you of a great impending punishment!" Abu Lahab then exclaimed, "It is for this that you have called us? Perish you!" Thus God sent down, "Perish the hands of Abū Lahab and perish he." According to tradition, both Abū Lahab and his wife were bitter enemies of the Prophet Muḥammad and Islām and did all they could to oppose him and do him harm. For this reason, they are both included in this unequivocal condemnation.

In the name of God the All Merciful, the Compassionate

1. Perish the hands of Abū Lahab and perish he.

2. His wealth shall avail him not, nor what he had earned.*

3. He shall burn in a flaming fire,

4. and his wife, the carrier of firewood,*

5. around her neck is a rope of palm fiber.*

(v. 2) What he earned means his offspring, according to Ibn 'Abbās.

(v. 4) Three opinions have been expressed concerning the description of Abū Lahab's wife as a carrier of firewood. The first is that she will carry fuel in Hell to increase her husband's torment. The second is that the word firewood is here used metaphorically to mean her gossip and backbiting. Finally, some commentators took the verse literally to mean that she actually used to carry firewood. This is unlikely because she was a member of the Umayyad, a rich and prestigious clan of Quraysh.

(v. 5) The palm fiber rope has been interpreted to mean a rope of fire which she will bear around her neck in Hell. This was because she had a precious necklace which she vowed to sell and spend the proceeds on a campaign against Muḥammad. Another view is that she will carry an iron chain or heavy iron necklace around her neck in Hell which is here called a rope of palm fiber.

(١١١) سُورَةُ المَسَدِ مَكِّيَّة
وآياتها ٥ نزلت بعد الفاتحة

بِسْمِ اللهِ الرَّحْمَنِ الرَّحِيمِ

تَبَّتْ يَدَاۤ أَبِي لَهَبٍ وَتَبَّ ﴿١﴾ مَاۤ أَغْنَى عَنْهُ مَالُهُ وَمَا
كَسَبَ ﴿٢﴾ سَيَصْلَى نَارًا ذَاتَ لَهَبٍ ﴿٣﴾ وَامْرَأَتُهُ حَمَّالَةَ
الْحَطَبِ ﴿٤﴾ فِي جِيدِهَا حَبْلٌ مِنْ مَسَدٍ ﴿٥﴾

Sūrah 112
al-Ikhlās
(Sincere Faith)

This *sūrah* consists of five verses and was revealed in Mecca after *sūrah* 114, *al-Nās*. It may be regarded as the creed of Islām. It contains a negation of *shirk* (association of other things or beings with God) in all its kinds. Hence God negated in Himself all kinds of multiplicity in His saying, 'God is the [unique] One.' He negated all kinds of needs or wants in His saying, 'God is the Eternal Refuge.' He negated all kinds of commonality of species or resemblance with any other beings in saying, 'He did not beget,' and negated coming into being or having a beginning in His saying, 'Nor was He begotten.' He finally negated any equals to Him in His saying, 'Nor is there anyone equal to Him'''.

It is related concerning the occasion of the revelation of this *sūrah* that the Meccan Associators sent to the Prophet a man called 'Āmir b. al-Ṭufayl who reproached him saying, "You have spread discord among us! You have insulted our gods and opposed the faith of your forefathers. If you do this because you are poor, we can make you rich. If you are possessed, we can cure you. If you do this because you love a particular woman, we shall give her to you in marriage." The Prophet replied, "I am neither poor nor possessed, nor have I fallen in love with a woman. I am the messenger of God sent to call you to worship Him instead of idols." The people sent 'Āmir a second time to the Prophet with the query, "Tell us of what the God you worship is made. Is He made of gold or silver?" Thus God sent down this *sūrah*.

The present *sūrah* is one of the most beloved portions of the Qur'ān. A number of traditions tell us that whoever loves this *sūrah*, God would love him and make him enter Paradise. There are many traditions asserting it to be equal to one-third or one-half of the Qur'ān. Thus the faithful are urged to recite it as often as they can, hundreds of times in one day and night. It is also recommended that this *sūrah* be recited on entering one's house or commencing any activity.

In the name of God the All Merciful, the Compassionate

1. Say: God, He is the One.
2. God is the eternal refuge.
3. He did not beget,
4. nor was He begotten.
5. Nor is there anyone equal to Him.

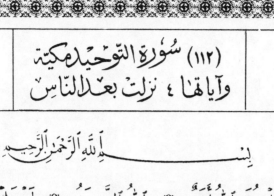

(١١٢) سُورةِ التّوحيدِمكيّة
وآياتها ٤ ، نزلت بعدالنّاس

بِسْمِ ٱللَّهِ ٱلرَّحْمَنِ ٱلرَّحِيمِ

قُلْ هُوَ ٱللَّهُ أَحَدٌ ﴿١﴾ ٱللَّهُ ٱلصَّمَدُ ﴿٢﴾ لَمْ يَلِدْ وَلَمْ يُولَدْ ﴿٣﴾ وَلَمْ يَكُن لَّهُۥ كُفُوًا أَحَدٌۢ ﴿٤﴾

Sūrah 113
al-Falaq
(Daybreak)

and

Sūrah 114
al-Nās
(Humankind)

This and the following *sūrah, al-Nās,* are known as the *al-Mu'awwidhatayn* (the two *sūrahs* of refuge). They and the previous *sūrah* are believed by pious people to have special blessings, a healing power and protection against evil. These two *sūrahs* especially have been used to ward off evil, even by the Prophet himself who recommended that they be recited as protection against illness and the envy of an evil eye. It is perhaps for this reason that Ibn Mas'ūd did not include them in his *mushaf* (collection of the Qur'ān). It is said that when he was asked about this, he answered, "The Apostle of God commanded us to recite them as protection from evil ... They are never part of the Book of God." It is, however, argued by other traditionists that, since they both begin with the command to the Prophet, "Say," it must be assumed that they were revealed as part of the Qur'ān. It is related that Ubayy b. Ka'b said, "We asked the Apostle of God concerning them and he said, 'It was said to me "Say" and I said.'" From the beginning, the Muslim community accepted these two *sūrahs* as part of the Qur'ān, relying on a widely accepted tradition, related with many chains of transmission, which asserts that the Apostle of God said, "Do you not see that tonight were sent down verses the like of which were never seen before: 'Say: I take refuge in the Lord of daybreak ...' [*sūrah* 113] and 'I take refuge in the Lord of humankind ...' [*sūrah* 114]"

The two *sūrahs* together consist of eleven verses. They are prayers for protection from all manner of human or nonhuman evil. They express God's sovereignty over all his Creation, and human confidence in his providential care. Commentators are not unanimous regarding the date or place of their revelation. The most widely accepted view is that they were both revealed in Mecca. Some have, however, asserted that they belong to the Medinan period of revelation.

Sūrah 113 al-Falaq (Daybreak)

In the name of God the All Merciful, the Compassionate

1. Say: I take refuge in the Lord of daybreak,*

2. from the evil of what He created;

3. from the evil of the darkness of night when it gathers;

4. from the evil of the women who blow on knots;*

5. from the evil of an envier when he envies.

(v. 1) The word *falaq*, although usually understood as "daybreak," has also been interpreted to mean "all creation". It is everything which God splits apart, such as the earth which is split by plants, the mountains which are split by water springs, the clouds which are split by the rainwaters and the wombs which open to bring forth children. Others understood the word *falaq* to refer to a special circle or well in Hell. Most commentators, however, prefer the first interpretation.

(v. 4) i.e. witches who spit and blow on knots for the purpose of causing their victims physical or psychological harm. The modern rationalist school of the late nineteenth and early twentieth century, however, rejected this classical view. According to a number of modern thinkers, it is the evil of the backbiter who seeks to sever the bond of love and separate loving people from one another. Thus their action is likened to blowing and the bond of love to a knot. This is because Arabs call the close bond between two things a knot, as the bond of spouses is called the knot of marriage. Gossip turns the love between two people into hostility by hidden means resembling a sort of magic.

(١١٣) سُورَةُ الْفَلَقِ مَكِّيَّة
وَآيَاتُهَا ٥ نزلت بعد الفيل

بِسْمِ اللَّهِ الرَّحْمَنِ الرَّحِيمِ

قُلْ أَعُوذُ بِرَبِّ الْفَلَقِ ﴿١﴾ مِن شَرِّ مَا خَلَقَ ﴿٢﴾ وَمِن شَرِّ

غَاسِقٍ إِذَا وَقَبَ ﴿٣﴾ وَمِن شَرِّ النَّفَّاثَاتِ فِي الْعُقَدِ ﴿٤﴾

وَمِن شَرِّ حَاسِدٍ إِذَا حَسَدَ ﴿٥﴾

Sūrah 114 al-Nās (Humankind)

   In the name of God the All Merciful, the Compassionate

1. Say: I take refuge in the Lord of humankind,

2. the King of humankind,

3. the God of humankind—

4. from the slinking whisperer,

5. who whispers in the breasts of men,

6. and of the jinn and men.*

(v. 6) There are two interpretations of this verse. Some commentators understood it to mean that the slinking whisperer whispers in the breasts of both jinn and men. Others, say that it means that there are whisperers among both jinn and men. According to tradition, every human being has his own Satan to test his faith and steadfastness.

(١١٤) سُورَة النَّاس مَكِّيَّة
وَآيَاتُهَا ٦ نَزَلَتْ بَعْدَ الْفَلَقَ

بِسْمِ اللهِ الرَّحْمَنِ الرَّحِيمِ

قُلْ أَعُوذُ بِرَبِّ النَّاسِ ۝ مَلِكِ النَّاسِ ۝
إِلَهِ النَّاسِ ۝ مِن شَرِّ الْوَسْوَاسِ الْخَنَّاسِ ۝
الَّذِي يُوَسْوِسُ فِي صُدُورِ النَّاسِ ۝ مِنَ الْجِنَّةِ
وَالنَّاسِ ۝

165

Appendix
al-Fātiḥah
(The Opening)

This *sūrah* was revealed in Mecca and consists of seven verses. The *sūrah* is known by many titles. The first is *al-Fātiḥah* (The Opening), because with it the Qur'ān opens, and with it the prayers begin. It is also known as *Umm al-Kitāb* (Mother of the Book), because it contains the essence of the Qur'ān. It is a summary of all the teachings of the Qur'ān, which were then detailed in the rest of the Book. This may be seen in the fact that the Qur'ān contains the profession of Divine Oneness *(tawḥīd)*. It also contains the promise for those who live by this faith of good reward, and the threat, for those who abandon it, of severe punishment. It teaches the kind of worship which enlightens (this faith) in the hearts and confirms it in the souls. The Qur'ān further guides to the way of happiness in this and the next world. It recounts the stories of those who abide by the laws and bounds which God set forth for his servants ... All these ideas are expressed in essence in *Sūrat al-Fātiḥah*.

The *Fātiḥah* is also known as *al-Sab' al-Mathani* ("the twice-repeated seven verses"), because it is repeated in the prayers. Other titles are: *al-Ḥamd* (the *sūrah* of praise) and *al-Ṣalāt* (the prayer). It is also called *al-Shifā'* (the *sūrah* of healing) and *al-Wāqiyah* (the *sūrah* of protection). It is the foundation (*Asās*) of the Qur'ān and *al-Kāfiyah* (the sufficient one).

Because of its great significance, *al-Fātiḥah* is not assigned with certainty to any specific period or place of revelation. Thus some commentators asserted that it was revealed in Medina. Still others held the view that it was revealed twice, in Mecca and in Medina. It is for this reason also that Ibn Mas'ūd did not include it in his *muṣḥaf*. When asked why, he answered, "Were I to write it, I would have to do so at the beginning of every *sūrah*." This is because it is repeated before any other *sūrah* in the prayers. Ibn Mas'ud continued, "I saw no need to write it down, since all Muslims memorize it."

The *Fātiḥah* is considered to be the greatest *sūrah* of the Qur'ān. The Prophet is said to have told Ubayy b. Ka'b that, "The like of the *Fātiḥah* was not sent down in the Torah, the Gospel or the Qur'ān". It is further reported from Abū Hurayrah that the Prophet said, "Whoever performs any prayers without

166

reciting in them the Mother of the Qur'ān, his prayers shall be incomplete [He repeated this three times]''.

Any recitation of the Qur'ān, except in prayer, must begin with the *isti'ādhah,* or the formula of refuge: "I take refuge in God from the accursed Satan." There are a number of verses in the Qur'ān which enjoin Muslims to seek refuge in God from the accursed Satan (see, for instance, 7: 200 and 16: 98). The word *shayṭān* (satan) has been derived by commentators from the verb *shaṭana* (meaning: to be removed far away). Thus Shayṭān is one who is far removed from the Good. The Qur'ān applies the term as an epithet to evil human beings, jinn and other evil spirits (see Qur'ān 6: 112.)

(I take refuge in God from the accursed Satan.)

1. In the name of God, the All-merciful, the Compassionate.*

2. All praise be to God, the Lord of all beings.*

3. The All-merciful, the Compassionate.

4. Master of the Day of Judgement.*

(v. 1) Commentators have differed regarding the *basmalah* (invocation of *bismillāh*). According to some, it is a verse of every *sūrah* except *sūrah* nine, where it does not occur. According to others, it is an independent verse placed at the beginning of every *sūrah* to separate it from the one after it. Still others held the *basmalah* to be a verse only of the *Fātiḥah*. Jurists have also differed as to whether the *basmalah* is to be recited aloud, or silently in the prayers.

The word *Allāh* in *bismillāh* is the name of God, all other names being attributes. According to some commentators, it is the greatest name of God. The words *Raḥmān* and *Raḥīm* are here rendered "All-merciful" and "Compassionate" because *Raḥmān* is an intensive form of the verb *raḥama*, signifying general mercy. *Raḥīm* signifies mercy toward the individual especially on the Day of Resurrection.

(v. 2) The word *ḥamd* (all praise) signifies both praise and thankfulness to God, whom the verse declares the absolute Lord of all beings. It is reported that the Prophet told his companions about a servant of God who praised God with the words, "O my Lord, all praise be to You as befits the majesty of your Face and the greatness of your Sovereignity." The man's two guardian angels did not know how to record the reward for this saying. God said to them, "Write it down just as my servant has uttered it until he meets me; then will I reward him for it". This utterance of praise is a source of great merit for those who proclaim it with sincerity.

(v. 4) Commentators have read this verse in two ways. Some read the word *mālik* as "master" and others as *mālik* (king). The word *mālik* means owner or master of all things on the Day of Judgment. The word *mālik* means king or sovereign over all things on the Day of Judgment. Both readings are equally acceptable and may be supported by other verses of the Qur'ān. The first reading is, however, more widely used because it was the reading of Mecca and Medina.

(١) سُورَةُ الفَاتِحَة
مَكِّيَّةٌ وَآيَاتُهَا سَبْع

بِسْمِ ٱللَّهِ ٱلرَّحْمَٰنِ ٱلرَّحِيمِ ﴿١﴾

ٱلْحَمْدُ لِلَّهِ رَبِّ ٱلْعَٰلَمِينَ ﴿٢﴾ ٱلرَّحْمَٰنِ ٱلرَّحِيمِ ﴿٣﴾

مَٰلِكِ يَوْمِ ٱلدِّينِ ﴿٤﴾ إِيَّاكَ نَعْبُدُ وَإِيَّاكَ نَسْتَعِينُ ﴿٥﴾

5. You alone do we worship, and You alone do we beseech for help.

6. Guide us on the straight way.*

7. The way of those upon whom You have bestowed your favour, not of those who have incurred your wrath or those who have gone astray.*

(v. 6) Commentators interpreted the words *al-ṣirāṭ al-mustaqīm* (straight way) in several ways. The first view is that *al-ṣirāṭ* is the Book of God; this is reported on the authority of 'Alī. According to Ibn 'Abbās and other Companions, the straight way means Islām. It is reported that the Prophet said, "God struck a similitude—a *ṣirāṭ*, on both sides of which are two walls with many open doors. Over the doors are curtains drawn. At the entrance of the *ṣirāṭ* stands a cryer calling out, "O people, enter onto the *ṣirāṭ*, all of you, and do not waver!' Another cryer, standing above the *ṣirāṭ*, calls out to anyone wishing to open one of the doors, 'Alas for you! Do not open it, for if you do, you would be lost therein!' The *ṣirāṭ* is Islām; the two high walls are the bounds of God, and the open doors are the sanctions and prohibitions of God. The cryer standing at the door of the *ṣirāṭ* is the Book of God, and the one over it is that [conscience] which God placed in the heart of every Muslim to admonish him". The *ṣirāṭ* may also be interpreted to mean Islām as the primordial faith which God placed as the *fiṭrah* (pure innate faith) in the heart of every human being.

(v. 7) Those who have found favour with God are, according to the Qur'ān, the Prophets, Truthful Ones, the Martyrs and the Righteous (see Qur'ān, 4: 69). Commentators have differed as to who are those who have incurred God's wrath and those who have gone astray. Most classical commentators, even though they interpret these words in a broad sense, still identified the first with the Jews and the second with the Christians. A more generally accepted view is that the verse refers to those who have incurred God's wrath are they who knew about the true religion, which God promulgated for his servants, yet rejected it. They are those who turn away from the consideration of proofs (that is, both in revelation and nature) which God established for humankind. Instead, they go on imitating the ways which they have inherited from their fathers and forefathers. As for those who have gone astray, they are the ones who did not know the truth, or at least did not know it in the right way. They are those who did not receive a divine message, or that it came to them in a way which did not help them to see the truth as it is. Such people are lost in their blindness, unable to be guided aright. They are engulfed by errors which confuse falsehood with truth and right with wrong. Thus if they are in error in the affairs of this world, they are also in error concerning those of the next.

170

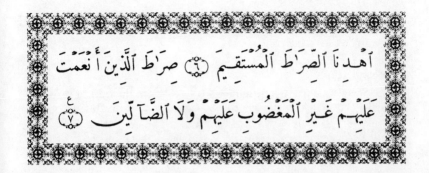

اهْدِنَا ٱلصِّرَٰطَ ٱلْمُسْتَقِيمَ ۝ صِرَٰطَ ٱلَّذِينَ أَنْعَمْتَ عَلَيْهِمْ غَيْرِ ٱلْمَغْضُوبِ عَلَيْهِمْ وَلَا ٱلضَّآلِّينَ ۝

Glossary

abtar: Derived from the verb *batara*, meaning to cut off, hence, and *abtar* is one who is cut off from society, because he left no offspring to carry on his name.

'Ād: The name of a tribe of ancient Arabia. God sent to this tribe the prophet Hūd.

adha: Means sacrifice and with the word *'id* refers to the feast of sacrifice at the end of the Pilgrimage Rite. *'id al-adha* is one of the two main Muslim festivals, the other being *'id al-fitr*, at the end of Ramadān.

ahruf: Singular of *harf*, meaning letter of the alphabet or mode or dialect. It is in this latter meaning that the word here is used.

'aqara : A verb meaning to hamstring or wound an animal, here used to refer to the slaying of the she-camel of the prophet Ṣāliḥ by the men of Thamūd.

Anṣār: Derived from the verb *nasara*, meaning to give support in times of hardship or war. The word here refers to the helpers, that is the inhabitants of Medina, who assisted Muḥammad and his companions when they migrated to the new city.

'aqabah: Means a steep road or hard space to traverse.

'Arafāt: The name of the mountain of sacrifice outside Mecca where pilgrims gather on the day before the feast of sacrifice.

asbāb: Singular of *Sabab*, meaning reason or occasion. The word is here used to mean occasions of the revelation [*nuzul*] of the Qur'ān.

Badr: The name of a famous spot; the Well of *Badr*, where the Muslims fought their first major and decisive battle against the Quraysh of Mecca.

bashshara: Meaning to give glad tidings. The word is used in the Qur'ān sometimes mockingly. That is, to announce to the rejectors of faith their impending punishment.

basmalah: Is a verbal constuct of the invocation *bismallah*.

burj: Singular of *burūj*, meaning heavenly stations, constellations or signs of the zodiac.

darī': Meaning dried, perhaps poisonous, thorny cactus, which grows in the desert. It will be the food of the rejectors of faith in hell.

Dhū al-Ḥijjah: Month of the Pilgrimage and last month of the Muslim calendar.

falaq: Derived from the verb *falaqa*, meaning to split open. It is God, who splits open the darkness by the light of day, hence the word means daybreak.

fath: Derived from the verb *fataha*, meaning to open or conquer.

fatrah: Derived from the verb *fatara*, meaning to cease or be interrupted. The word means interruption of undetermined duration.

fitr: Derived from the verb *aftara*, meaning to break a fast. The word is generally used to refer to the breaking of the fast of Ramadān.

fitrah: Derived from the *fatara*, meaning to create or originate. The word here means the state of a human individual as God originally created him, pure and innocent.

furqān: Derived from the verb *faraqa*, meaning to separate or distinguish. The word here means the criterion by which truth and falsehood may be distinguished. It is one of the names or titles of the Qur'ān.

hadīth: Derived from the verb *haddatha*, meaning to report, tell or narrate an event or opinion. The word is commonly used to refer to the sayings of the Prophet.

hāfirah: Derived from the verb *hafara*, meaning to dig a pit or trench. The word is used here to mean the grave or life in the grave.

hijrah: Derived from the verb *hajara*, meaning to migrate, runaway or desert. Here the word signifies the migration of the Prophet and his companions [*muhājirūn*] from Mecca to Medina. The hijrah marks the beginning of Muslim history.

Hūd: Name of a Messenger who was sent to the tribe of '*Ād*. The tribe rejected him and was destroyed.

hamd: Means praise. Here used as a name for the *Fātihah*, because after the invocation, "In the name of God ...", the *surāh* begins with the word of praise.

hunafā': Plural of *hanif*, meaning to be a person or persons of pure faith. The term *hanif* is used in the Qur'ān to describe Abraham.

'īd: Means a festival or feast day.

Iram: The name of the ancestor of the tribe of '*Ād*.

isti'ādhah: Derived from the verb *'awadha*, meaning to seek refuge or protection. The word means here seeking refuge in God.

kāfiyah: Derived from the verb *kafaya*, meaning to suffice. The word is used here to indicate that the *Fātihah* is sufficient for the pious.

katabat: Derived from the verb *kataba*, meaning to write down or inscribe. It is the plural of the word *katib*, meaning writer or scribe, and here refers to the scribes of revelation [*katabat al wahī*].

khalīfah: Derived from the verb *khalafa*, meaning to succeed or represent. The word is commonly used to designate the Muslim rulers, who succeeded the prophet Muhammad.

khatm: Derived from the verb *khatama*, meaning to seal or complete. Here the word means completion of an entire recitation of the Qur'ān.

kufr: Derived from the verb *kafara*, meaning to cover or obscure. The word here is rendered as "rejection of faith" to signify knowledge and willfull rejection.

173

laylat al-qadr: The night of determination; some have interpreted the word *qadr* to mean "power" derived from the verb *qadara*, meaning to be able or have power. Here it is derived from the verb *qaddra*, meaning to determine. This is the more correct derivation for this context.

mā'ūn: Means vessel or utensil, but when derived from the verb *a'āna* means to give assistance in time of need.

mālik: Derived from the verb *malaka*, meaning to own or possess. Thus, the word means owner or master, that is one possessing absolute control.

malik: Is another form derived from the verb *malaka*, meaning king.

mathānī: The word means dual or two things. Here it is used to mean twice repeated verses, because the *Fātiḥah* is repeated twice in every prayer.

Mīna: One of the important stations of Pilgrimage outside Mecca.

mi'rāj: Derived from the verb *'araja*, meaning to ascend, here used as a noun, meaning ascension. This refers to the night journey and ascension to heaven of the Prophet.

Mu'awwidhatayn: This is the name for the two last *sūrahs* of the Qur'ān. They are so called, because they both begin with the formula of refuge.

mudabbirāt: Derived from the verb *dabbara*, meaning to direct or manage an affair. The word here as used in the plural to refer to angels who manage the affairs of this world or to the stars, including the sun and moon.

Muḥarram: The sacred month and first month of the Muslim year.

muṣḥaf: Derived from the verb *ṣahafa*, meaning to write things in scrolls or on large sheets of paper or parchment. The word is commonly used to designate a written copy of the Qur'ān.

mustaqīm: Derived from the verb *qawama*, meaning to make straight. The word, therefore means straight without any crookedness, and when signifying human conduct implies rectitude and honesty.

Muzdalifah: The name of a spot below Mt. 'Arafāt where the pilgrims go after their gathering on Mt. 'Arafāt.

na'īm: Derived from the verb *na'ima*, meaning to be in a state bliss, happiness or comfort. The word is also used as a name for Paradise.

nāmūs: Perhaps derived from the Greek word *nomos*, meaning law, here used to refer to the Law or Torah of Moses.

nās: The word means people in the general sense.

nāshiṭat: Derived from the verb *nashata*, meaning to engage in intense activity or be filled with sudden energy. The word used here in the plural to refer to the angels of death throwing the souls vehemently from their bodies or to the stars rising swiftly in their orbits.

naskh: Derived from the verb *nasakha*, meaning to abolish or abrogate. Here it is used to refer to the abrogation of verses of the Qur'ān.

nāzi'āt: Derived from the verb *naza'a*, meaning to pluck out, extract or rush on. The word is used here to refer to angels extracting the souls of human beings from their bodies or to the stars rising swiftly.

qirā'āt: Derived from the verb qara'a, meaning to read or recite. *Qirā'āt* is the plural of the word *qrā'ah*, meaning reading or recitation. The word here refers to the various readings of the Qur'ān.

rādifah: Derived from the verb *radafa*, meaning to be like something that happened previously or be the second of two similar things. The word is used here to describe the second quaking of the earth or heaven.

Raḥīm: Is another form derived from the verb *Raḥama.* It signifies God's mercy towards each individual creature, hence, the rendering "Compassionate".

Raḥmān: Derived from the verb *Raḥama*, meaning to show mercy. The word is an intensive form of this verb, denoting God's general mercy for all His creation, for this reason it is here translated "All Merciful".

rājifah: Derived from the verb *rajafa*, meaning to shake, quake or shiver. The word is used here to designate the quaking of the earth on the day of resurrection.

rak'ah: Derived from the verb *raka'a*, meaning to kneel or bow down. The word means a specific unit in the cycle of prayers.

riddah: Derived from the verb *radda*, meaning to return. The word here refers to Muslims, who after the death of the Prophet, decided to return to their original faith and customs.

sab': means seven. Here used to designate the seven verses of the opening *surah* of the Qur'ān.

sāhirah: Derived from the verb *sahira*, meaning to wake up or stay up at night. The word may also mean the flat smooth earth on which people will be gathered on the day of resurrection.

salāt: Means prayers as worship, specifically, the five daily prayers.

Ṣaliḥ: One of the ancient messengers of God to the tribe of Thamūd.

Shaf': Meaning the even number either of prayers or created things in pairs.

shahādah: Derived from the verb *shahida*, meaning to bear witness, here used as a noun to mean the profession of faith or witness that, "There is no god, but God and that Muhammad is the apostle of God."

sharī'ah: Meaning the sacred law of Islām. The word literally means a highway or bank of a river, that is something to be followed or turned to.

shifā': Means healing, here used to signify both physical and spiritual healing.

Shayṭān: Derived by classical commentators from the verb *shatana*, meaning to be removed far away, in this case, from all good. The word in reality is of uncertain origin.

shirk: Derived from the verb *ashraka*, meaning to assign a partner or associate. Here it is used as a noun, meaning association of other things or beings with God.

sijjin: Derived from the verb *sajana*, meaning to imprison. The word *sijjin* is an intensive form of this verb. It means a low place from which there is no escape.

ṣirāṭ: Derived from the verb *ṣaraṭa*, meaning to swallow. The word, thus signifies a highway which swallows a traveler out of sight.

sūrah: according to most commentators *sūrah* is derived from the word *sūr*, meaning wall or enclosure (e.g.) around a city. It refers to a portion of the Qur'ān made up of three verses or more and separated from other portions.

takbīr: Derived from the verb *kabbra*, meaning to magnify or proclaim the greatness of something. Here used as a noun for the phrase "*allāhu akbar*" [God is most Great].

tasnīm: Means a spring of water or stream descending from a high place. Here it refers to a special spring of paradisial water from which the faithful will drink.

tawḥīd: Derived from the verb *waḥḥada*, meaning to proclaim the oneness of God. The word commonly means proclaimation of, or faith in the 'one and only God'.

Thamūd: The name of a tribe which lived in Arabia long before Islām, and to whom God sent the prophet Ṣāliḥ.

'usr: Means hardship or difficulty.

waḥī: Means direct revelation through an angel to a prophet to be distinguished from inspiration [*ilhām*] which is possible for every person.

wāqiyah: Derived from the verb *waqaya*, meaning to protect or defend. The word is used here to signify that the Fātiḥah is a protection against evil.

watr: Meaning the odd number of days or created things. It may also refer to night prayers.

yusr: means ease, comfort and good fortune. It is the opposite of *'usr*.

zakāt: Means the act of almsgiving. It is, however, specified tax on savings or property to be given for the poor as an act of religious purification.